Zemlinsky Studies

Edited by Michael Frith

Zemlinsky Studies

Edited by Michael Frith

First published in 2007 by Middlesex University Press

Copyright © Middlesex University Department of Music

Authors retain copyright of individual chapters.

ISBN 978 1 904750 18 5

A CIP catalogue record for this book is available from The British Library

Cover design by Helen Taylor
Typesetting by Carnegie Publishing Ltd
Printed in the UK by Cromwell Press

Published in association with:

Alexander Zemlinsky
Fonds
bei der
Gesellschaft der Musikfreunde
in Wien

Cover picture
Richard Gerstl Portrait *Alexander von Zemlinsky*, 1907, oil on canvas, 170.5 x 74.3 cm, Stiftung Sammlung Kamm, Kunsthaus Zug
Photograph: Alfred Frommenwiler

Middlesex University Press
North London Business Park
Oakleigh Road South
London N11 1QS
Tel: +44 (0)20 8411 4162: +44 (0)20 8411 4161
Fax: +44 (0)20 8411 4167
www.mupress.co.uk

Contents

Acknowledgements

THE EDITOR WOULD LIKE to thank the contributors to this book, first for their original participation in the Zemlinsky symposium at Middlesex University and second for their enthusiasm, efficiency and promptness in recasting their papers for publication against a tight schedule; in particular to Peter Fribbins and Christopher Dromey for organising the symposium (ably assisted by Barbra Back, Music Administrator at Middlesex University), and for their invaluable assistance in the preparation of the book; Mine Dogantan Dack, Research Fellow in Music, Middlesex University, has been a source of encouragement and help. Thanks are also due to those who performed at the symposium: Shoko Hino, Jane Manning, Terence Allbright, Raphael Wallfisch and John York. Financial assistance has kindly been given by the Zemlinsky Fonds of Vienna (*Alexander Zemlinsky Fonds bei der Gesellschaft der Musikfreunde in Wien*), the Director of which, Peter Dannenberg, has provided a Foreword and to Silvia Kargl who has given invaluable help and advice. The editor also gratefully acknowledges permission granted by copyright holders to reproduce material as detailed in the text. Tribute must also be paid to Celia Cozens, Managing Editor, Middlesex University Press, and her staff for their efficiency, forbearance and untiring encouragement at every stage in the preparation of the volume.

Michael Frith
Middlesex University

Preface

THE DISCOVERY OF THE score of Zemlinsky's early Sonata for Cello and Piano and its subsequent editing and performance were major events for scholars and admirers of its composer. The essays presented in this book originated as papers given at a one-day symposium hosted by Middlesex University in October 2006; most of them are revised and expanded versions of the original papers, though others, such as that by Philip Weller, pursue rather different lines of thought. In general, the editorial policy has been to preserve the identity and individual character of each contribution as far as possible with the minimum of editorial intervention. There is naturally a certain amount of overlapping between different contributions, but extensive cross-referencing is hardly necessary in such a relatively slim volume.

The symposium culminated in a recital by Raphael Wallfisch and John York in which the Sonata received its UK première, along with two other early pieces for cello and piano, and a recent Sonata by Peter Fribbins, who gives his view of Zemlinsky's String Quartets in this volume. The keynote address at the symposium was given by Antony Beaumont, who is not only the editor of the recently discovered Sonata and of numerous other works by Zemlinsky, but also the author of the authoritative biography of the composer. Beaumont is also well known as a conductor, particularly in Germany, for his interpretations of Zemlinsky's music. His chapter in this book is an amplified version of his keynote paper: here, he discusses the problems of editing the Sonata and gives a detailed account of the editing of other works. This throws interesting light, *inter alia,* on the changing attitudes of the composer's widow towards his works and his memory.

The first two chapters are largely biographical. Raymond Coffer's researches have revealed some fascinating details of a previously little-known period (1907–8) in the lives of the recently married Zemlinskys, Schoenberg and his wife Mathilde (née Zemlinsky), and the painter Richard Gerstl, who committed suicide shortly after the discovery of his affair with Mathilde. Coffer's subtle and detailed analysis of several of Gerstl's paintings sheds light on the deteriorating relationships within the extended family and illuminates what was for Schoenberg a decisive stage in his development as a composer. Zemlinsky's reputation in his lifetime was very largely tied up with his activities as a conductor; nowhere was this more apparent than in his period in Prague, where he was appointed chief conductor of the New German

Theatre in 1911. Pamela Tancsik and David Smith discuss Zemlinsky's work there, and, in the contexts of his often difficult relationships with the theatre's management and wider political issues, explore his determined and unstinting services to new opera and to those composers upon whose works he lavished such careful and detailed attention. Zemlinsky's generosity towards his contemporaries is one of the outstanding features of his character and sometimes appears, perhaps deceptively, to have inhibited his development as a composer.

Philip Weller takes Adorno's well-known article *Zemlinsky*[1] as the starting point for a detailed enquiry into Zemlinsky's relationship to his predecessors and contemporaries, and asks the question why Adorno, with his radically Marxist orientation, should have felt so strongly about the significance of music such as Zemlinksy's (and that of Schreker, too), and why he felt it necessary to write the article in the first place. Weller shows, through a close reading of Adorno's text and by relating it to some of his other writings, not only that Adorno's approach could be surprisingly pluralistic, but that Zemlinsky was more radical as a composer than is often supposed; this can be seen particularly in such works as the Third String Quartet, Op. 19 (1924) and the *Sinfonietta*, Op. 23 (1934). Moreover, his dual focus as both performer and composer, within a long-established Austro-German tradition, was, Weller argues, a strength, and Zemlinsky's devotion to his performing repertoire actually nourished his creative powers.

The last four essays focus on analytical issues: Shoko Hino draws attention to the many nineteenth-century influences to be found within Zemlinsky's early *Fantasies* Op. 9, whilst noting those features which were characteristic of the emerging new styles associated with expressionism; she finds an individual voice in precisely the way Zemlinsky holds disparate traits in equilibrium. Christopher Dromey analyses the structure and content of the unfinished *Maiblumen blühten überall* for soprano and string sextet, and draws some interesting conclusions concerning its relationship to its predecessors in the sextet medium and to Schoenberg's *Verklärte Nacht*; his essay ends by speculating that further development of the sextet medium was overtaken by a growing preoccupation with mixed, heterogeneous ensembles. Steven Vande Moortele and Peter Fribbins concentrate on Zemlinsky's String Quartets: on the Second and its relationship to what had become an established tradition of what Moortele terms 'two dimensional' sonata form; and the First and Fourth, on which Fribbins gives his perspective as a composer, particularly of chamber music. Performances of Zemlinsky's works were a prominent feature of the symposium, and in an appendix we include an edited text of a stimulating lecture–recital given by Jane Manning (soprano) and Terence Allbright (piano).

Despite one or two minor revivals of interest, Zemlinsky has never attained the recognition which the quality of his music merits. Several contributors in this volume refer to Adorno's well-known essay in his *Quasi una fantasia* and his charge of eclecticism:

The presence of eclectic features in the texture of his works cannot be denied; they reflect the conductor's love for the masterpieces of his age, a love from which sensibility is unable to draw back when he comes to compose. But of course, great works can scarcely be imagined without such love. An originality which is on a par with the achievements of the age, but does not spring from an intimate knowledge of what is essential to it, does not count. Just because music had been split up into particular intentions, each of which had its own validity, the task facing Zemlinsky's generation was one of unification.

Only now can we see that this task was incapable of fulfilment. But he faced up to it to the point of self-immolation with a musical intelligence devoid of all prejudice and preconception.[2]

Zemlinsky's case would appear to be an example of the phenomenon identified by Harold Bloom as the 'Anxiety of Influence', a theory of poetry which various commentators have found applicable to music and which involves an agonic contest between 'strong' and 'weak' poets. When the younger poet encounters the work of an older, strong poet, he:

> ...is condemned to learn his profoundest yearnings through an awareness of *other selves*. The poem is *within* him, yet he experiences the shame and splendour of *being found by* poems – great poems – *outside* him.[3]

He, too, then becomes a strong poet through the process of 'misreading' the precursor poet in order to 'clear imaginative space' for himself;[4] this involves one or more of Bloom's 'Six Revisionary Ratios', which include a swerving away from the original in the direction made apparently necessary by the new poet, or a completion, implying that the 'precursor had failed to go far enough'.[5] Bloom's central principle is that:

> Poetic Influence – when it involves two strong, authentic poets – always proceeds by a misreading of the prior poet, an act of creative correction that is actually and necessarily a misinterpretation. The history of fruitful poetic influence, which is to say the main tradition of Western poetry since the Renaissance, is a history of anxiety and self-saving caricature, of distortion, of perverse, wilful revisionism without which modern poetry as such could not exist.[6]

The strong poet – and the strong composer, therefore – must ruthlessly hold true to the narrowness and the perversity of their visions – their 'prejudice and preconception'. For 'in the last analysis the greatest talents require a fund of barbarism, however deeply buried. This was denied to Zemlinsky'.[7] Zemlinsky, it might appear, always stopped short of 'misreading' his precursors and his 'stronger' contemporaries, and he evaded the anxiety of any single influence by successively submitting himself to the influences of the very strong poets surrounding him; 'self-immolation'[8] is hardly characteristic of a strong poet.

If Shakespeare was, as Bloom suggests, the original strong poet of literature, Beethoven must be the equivalent in music; he epitomises the culture of the individual, of artistic progress, of the concepts of 'genius' and 'originality', of the fundamentally masculine aggression and assertiveness reflected in Bloom's unremittingly gendered language (significantly, even in the 1997 edition). In an earlier era, a Zemlinsky-like talent would almost certainly have had no problem in relation to either his precursors or his contemporaries, nor would the future have been a concern. His music would have taken its place among other products of its time and school. Bloom's theory maps well onto the historical trajectory of the German symphonic tradition from Beethoven to Brahms[9], but the increasing plurality of traditions and aesthetics already present in the Brahms/Wagner era, together with the fragmentation of musical languages and availability of alternative styles, meant that by the early twentieth century the influence of a single 'strong' composer no longer needed to be so oppressive. Finding a personal style and an individual voice from among a range of 'strong voices' became a far greater necessity – and even source of anxiety – for many composers. From an early twenty-first-century vantage point, we can see that posterity is already having second thoughts about the work and legacies of some of the 'strong' composers who were Zemlinsky's contemporaries, notably Schoenberg, whom Zemlinsky refused to follow into the wilderness of atonality and serialism. Nor is Zemlinsky's obvious eclecticism any longer seen as a disadvantage, for as Adorno presciently observed:

> ...his eclecticism shows genius in its truly seismographic sensitivity to the stimuli by which he allowed himself to be overwhelmed. Weakness which never pretends to be creative acquires the strength of a second nature. The unreserved sacrifice of the pathos of personality becomes a critique of personality and hence something intensely personal. Soft-heartedness, sensitivity, nervousness – all these result in something quite unmistakable.[10]

Almost half a century ago, Adorno envisioned the 'strong poet' of the future with qualities totally different from those of Bloom's world, qualities which we are at last beginning to recognise as virtues. Zemlinsky is still waiting, but the increasing desire to perform and experience his music, as evinced by the programme of the symposium in October 2006, and the enthusiasm for discussing and evaluating it – as demonstrated by the papers reproduced in this volume – are mounting evidence that his time cannot be long in coming.

Notes

1   Adorno, TW (1963/1992) *Quasi una Fantasia. Essays on Modern Music* (trans. R
    Livingstone). London and New York: Verso, pp.111–29. It was first published in German
    in 1963 and was reprinted in Adorno, TW (1997) *Gesammelte Schriften,* (ed. Rolf
    Tiedemann), 20 vols. Frankfurt am Main: Suhrkamp-Taschenbuch Wissenschaft, vol. 16,
    pp.351–67.
2   Ibid. pp.114–15
3   Bloom, H (1973/1997) *The Anxiety of Influence: A Theory of Poetry.* New York and Oxford:
    Oxford University Press, p.26.
4   Ibid., p.5
5   Ibid., pp.14–16
6   Ibid., p.30
7   Adorno, op. cit., p.127
8   Ibid., p.115
9   See Bonds, ME (1996) *After Beethoven: Imperatives of Originality in the Symphony.*
    Cambridge, Mass. and London: Harvard University Press.
10 Adorno, op. cit., p.1155   *Ibid.*, pp.14–16
6   *Ibid.*, p.30
7   Adorno, op. cit., p.127
8   *Ibid.*, p.115
9   *Ibid.*

Alexander von Zemlinsky

Born Vienna 14 October 1871
Died Larchmont New York 15 March 1942

Vorwort

BEIM EDINBURGH FESTIVAL 1983 wurden in einem Gastspiel der Hamburgischen Staatsoper Alexander von Zemlinskys Opern-Einakter „Eine florentinische Tragödie" und „Der Geburtstag der Infantin" (Der Zwerg) nach Texten von Oscar Wilde vorgestellt. In einer Londoner Besprechung der Aufführung hieß es, es gäbe keine unbekannten Meisterwerke, aber hier habe man zwei entdeckt. In der Tat war ja das musikalische Oeuvre Zemlinskys, vor allem bedingt durch die politischen Ereignisse in Österreich und Mitteleuropa in den dreißiger Jahren, völlig vergessen und wurden nicht mehr gespielt.

Erst von 1980 an kam es zur Wiederentdeckung des Komponisten, der inzwischen als wichtige Brücke zwischen später Romantik und neuer Musik wieder seinen festen Platz in den Opernhäusern und Konzertsälen gefunden hat – und auch die beiden in Edinburgh gespielten Opern haben ja wenig später auch Einzug in Covent Garden gehalten.

Der Alexander-Zemlinsky-Fonds ist glücklich darüber, dass sich nach den großen Symposien in Graz und Wien die Middlesex University als erste Institution in Großbritannien entschlossen hat, durch eine Tagung die wissenschaftliche Forschung über Person und Werk Zemlinskys zu vertiefen. Die Auswahl der Referenten, das breite Spektrum der Themen und die Qualität der Vorträge haben es verdient, über den Tag hinaus festgehalten und einem größeren interessierten Publikum bekannt gemacht zu werden.

Dazu mag diese Veröffentlichung dienen. Sie wird Veranstalter wie Publikum gewiß dazu anregen, sich vermehrt Zemlinskys Kammermusik, seinen Orchesterwerken und seinen Opern auch in Großbritannien zuzuwenden.

Peter Dannenberg
Erster Vorsitzender des Alexander-Zemlinsky-Fonds bei der Gesellschaft der Musikfreunde in Wien

Foreword

A T THE 1983 EDINBURGH Festival, the Hamburg State Opera presented
a guest performance of Alexander von Zemlinsky's single-act operas *Eine
florentinische Tragödie* and *Der Geburtstag der Infantin* (also known as
Der Zwerg) based on texts by Oscar Wilde. A London review of the performance
noted that there were thought to be no unknown masterpieces, but that here two
had been discovered. Indeed, due mainly to political events in Austria and Central
Europe during the 1930s, Zemlinsky's musical oeuvre was completely forgotten and
no longer performed.

Only since 1980 has the composer been rediscovered; once again he has found
his proper place in the opera houses and concert halls as an important bridge
between late Romantic and Modern music and, in fact, the two operas performed in
Edinburgh were staged shortly thereafter at Covent Garden.

After important symposia held in Graz and Vienna, the Alexander Zemlinsky
Foundation is delighted that Middlesex University was the first British institution
to organise a conference with the aim of extending scholarly research both about
Zemlinsky's works and his life. The choice of speakers, the broad range of themes,
and the quality of the presentations should be preserved for the future and presented
to a wider interested audience.

This publication will serve that purpose. It will surely inspire promoters of his
music as well as the English-speaking public to reappraise Zemlinsky's chamber
music, his orchestral works and operas.

Peter Dannenberg
President of the Alexander Zemlinsky Foundation at the Gesellschaft der
Musikfreunde (Friends of Music Society) in Vienna
Trans: Dr Ralf Nuhn, Research Fellow LCEA, Middlesex University

Raymond Coffer

Betwixt the Hof- and the Volksoper: a Portrait of Zemlinsky in Gmunden, 1908

WHILST THE BIOGRAPHY OF Alexander Zemlinsky has benefited from the existence of much detailed information, as beautifully brought together in Antony Beaumont's excellent book,[1] almost nothing is known of the key period in Zemlinsky's life, stretching from when he was forced to leave the Hofoper in February 1908 to his official return to the Volksoper in 1909. Even Beaumont, when asked whether he knew anything of Zemlinsky's activities during this time, replied 'I have little idea about this. Later in autumn 1908, he probably travelled to Mannheim for a few days. Other than that, there seems little to go on.'[2] However, what is certain is that Zemlinsky was witness to one of the most sensational and influential love affairs of *fin-de-siècle* Vienna, that between Zemlinsky's sister, Mathilde, wife of Zemlinsky's great friend and student, Arnold Schoenberg, and the young expressionist artist, Richard Gerstl. Now, however, as research into the affair reveals newly discovered documents, it is possible to fill in a few sketchy gaps about Zemlinsky's activities during 1908 and in the process give an insight into both the world inhabited by the Schoenberg and Zemlinsky families during that period, and the creative works that came out of it. Central to all this were a series of dramatic portraits of Schoenberg and his circle which Gerstl painted in Gmunden in July 1908, just weeks before the affair was exposed, one of which is Gerstl's *Portrait of Alexander Zemlinsky* (Fig. 1), which now resides in the Kunsthaus Zug as part of the 'Stiftung Sammlung Kamm'.

Zemlinsky, born in 1871, and Mathilde, born six years later, were so close that Zemlinsky had said that 'should the need arise, one of us would willingly make any sacrifice for the other.'[3] Having become Schoenberg's only teacher and possibly his closest friend,[4] it was hardly surprising that it was perhaps through her brother's matchmaking that Mathilde met Schoenberg in 1899, marrying him in October 1901. Indeed, on their return from Berlin in 1903, the Schoenbergs, together with their two-year-old daughter, Trude, were to become neighbours to Zemlinsky, moving into an adjoining apartment in 68/70 Liechtensteinstrasse, a recently built block in Vienna's upcoming 9th district (Fig. 2).

Fig. 1, Richard Gerstl Portrait *Alexander von Zemlinsky* oil on canvas 170.5 x 74.3 cm
Stiftung Sammlung Kamm, Kunsthaus Zug

Mathilde was pregnant with her second child, Georg, when, three years later, in spring 1906, Gerstl introduced himself to Schoenberg. He must have made an impression, for Schoenberg was quick to accede to the young man's offer to paint a large-scale portrait of the composer,[5] followed by one of Mathilde with her daughter.[6] Schoenberg was evidently satisfied with Gerstl's efforts, for, having identified portraiture as a useful means of income to relieve the financial pressures that blighted his life, he now invited Gerstl to teach him, and possibly Mathilde too, painting techniques.

Perhaps Schoenberg's lack of income had created disaffection within the marriage, but in any case, Mathilde was to reward Schoenberg by having a passionate affair with the 24-year-old Gerstl in the Upper Austrian spa of Gmunden, which culminated in a sensational denouement towards the end of the traditional summer break of 1908. Moreover, no sooner were the two lovers discovered than Mathilde chose to flee back to Vienna with Gerstl, eventually to be persuaded by Anton Webern to return to her family, a turn of events which was to be partially responsible for Gerstl committing suicide in his studio in November of that year. His method was to put a noose around his neck and stab himself in the heart. He was just 25.

This tragic, adulterous triangle must have been just one more disaster in 1908, Zemlinsky's 37th year, and a true *annus horribilis*. The year had started ominously badly. In the first place, Mahler's exit from the Hofoper, and his subsequent departure to New York in December 1907 had proved to be emotional and dispiriting moments, especially for Schoenberg and his students and, incidentally, for Gerstl too. For Zemlinsky it bordered on disaster as Zemlinsky, having finally made the leap from the Volksoper to the Hofoper in spring 1907, had not only received a new contract from Mahler, but had also had the premiere of his opera, *Der Traumgörge*, scheduled by the Director for 4 October 1907. It was Zemlinsky's misfortune that Mahler's own contract was officially terminated two days before *Traumgörge's* first night, with the result that Mahler's successor, Weingartner, promptly cancelled the performance.

Fig. 2, Arnold and Mathilde Schoenberg, with Trude and Georg, in their apartment, 68/70 Liechtensteinstrasse, *c.*1907, ASC

Fig. 3, Mathilde and Alexander Zemlinsky c.1886, Arnold Schönberg Center, Vienna ASC

Zemlinsky must have been devastated, for Weingartner had promised Mahler that the work would be staged. Worse, Zemlinsky received no further conducting duties, and, unwelcome and unwanted, with his position untenable, Zemlinsky took three months leave, eventually having his contract annulled on 15 February 1908. Mahler was sympathetic but powerless.

Returning with his tail between his legs, the Volksoper did provide Zemlinsky with temporary sanctuary, but only as a guest conductor, overseeing perhaps ten works in the back end of the spring 1908 season. However, by the end of May Zemlinsky, a workaholic and inveterate wage-earner, found himself unemployed, and whilst he sporadically conducted at the Volksoper in the following season, he was not invited back full time until the autumn of 1909. To compound his problems, on 8 May 1908, Zemlinsky became father to a daughter, Hansi, whose first weeks were a struggle against illness, which, to Zemlinsky's certain despair, was soon to manifest itself in deafness, and an inability to hear even her father's most lullaby-like music.

By now, Schoenberg had become suspicious of his wife's relationship with Gerstl, not least, perhaps, on account of Gerstl taking a studio above the Schoenbergs' apartment, which, despite Schoenberg's ban, Mathilde had apparently continued to visit. Thus, at the beginning of June 1908, Schoenberg removed Mathilde and their two children from Vienna and scuttled them off to Gmunden, ahead of his arrival at the end of the month. From here, Mathilde and Arnold conducted an almost daily correspondence,[7] which, whilst hinting at Schoenberg's suspicions of Gerstl and Mathilde, also provides some clues as to Zemlinsky's state of mind at the time.

Schoenberg and Zemlinsky had taken a liking to Gmunden (Fig. 4), and in the previous year, 1907, had rented farmhouses along the eastern side of the Traunsee, Schoenberg in number 22, and Zemlinsky and his new wife Ida in number 20. As neighbours, it was natural for the Schoenberg and Zemlinsky families to take their summer breaks together which, typical of Viennese culture, could last from June

Fig. 4, Postcard of
Gmunden, 1907,
private collection

Fig. 5, Postcard from *Feramühle*,
*c.*1900
Collection of Elfriede Prillinger, Gmunden

Fig. 6, Richard Gerstl, *Meadow with trees*,
Summer 1907
Oil on Canvas and Board, 36 x 38 cm
Stiftung Sammlung Kamm, Kunsthaus Zug

until September and often involved the shipment of crates of chattels and furniture out of the metropolis to country accommodation.

In 1907, Schoenberg had begun his habit of inviting his students to join him. Gerstl was asked to join, too, and found himself living 400 metres along the lakeside, under the Traunstein, at the *Feramühle* (Fig. 5). Gerstl, having viewed van Gogh's first solo Vienna show in January 1906, had evidently been impressed with the Dutchman's impressionism for, in summer 1907, Gerstl painted a series of extraordinary landscapes around the grounds of the *Feramühle* (see, for example, Fig. 6), which clearly display van Gogh's influence. Several of these paintings were to depict, perhaps deliberately, the very path, through the steep hillside orchards above the lake that Mathilde would eventually take to her lover, thus avoiding being spotted on the more commonly used lakeside embankment.

With Zemlinsky able to look forward to the forthcoming season at the Hofoper, the early portion of that 1907 holiday was particularly satisfying for the Zemlinskys. They had married on 21 June and, according to a postcard sent by Ida and Alex shortly after, had honeymooned in the Berchtesgaden area, enjoying the underground salt lakes.[8] More importantly, Ida's sister Melanie, a close friend of the Schoenbergs and Zemlinsky's girlfriend before Alma, also arrived on honeymoon from New York with her new American husband William Clark Rice who, in Gmunden in July 1907, was to paint the only known portrait of Gerstl,[9] other then Gerstl's own self-portraits.

Gerstl, still a student of the Academy at the time, appears to have been content on his first visit to Gmunden, writing to his brother in Vienna at the end of July 1907 that he had spent his time diligently producing sketches, probably the landscapes mentioned earlier, adding that he was getting along with his new friends from Vienna, presumably Messrs Schoenberg and Zemlinsky, very well indeed.[10] It has been suggested that Zemlinsky's portrait, together with others that were stylistically from the same period, including one said to portray Melanie and William Clark Rice,[11] was in fact painted in 1907. However, this is highly unlikely, for not only was Gerstl apparently concentrating on landscapes at the time and makes no mention of any portraits to his brother, but Rice had left Gmunden for Rome on July 27,[12] the same day as Gerstl's letter, and was therefore simply not around. Moreover, Zemlinsky left a few days later to rehearse *Tannhauser* and *Carmen* at the Hofoper,[13] which he then conducted on the 20 and 21 August. It is thus highly unlikely that Gerstl painted Zemlinsky's portrait in 1907, but almost certain that he did so, together with others in the series, in 1908.

For summer 1908, Schoenberg upgraded his Gmunden accommodation, staying just one farmhouse south along the lake, number 24, *Prestgütl*. This was rather nicer than the previous year's. It had its own rowing boat, the *Pepscherl*, and cows, which were milked each morning by the farmer so that fresh supplies were available for the guests. It was here that Schoenberg, who was forced to spend the rest of the year making a living teaching and correcting, would be able to calmly dedicate his time to composing. However, on this occasion, it was his intention to set aside July 1908 for the completion of the final three movements of his seminal Second String Quartet, Op. 10 which, in the fourth movement, crosses the bridge to atonality for the first time.

Zemlinsky on the other hand, either because of a lack of funds or the pressing needs of his newborn daughter, was clearly not himself, his mood in stark contrast to a year earlier. He had not even settled his summer accommodation, as Mathilde, acting as her brother's travel agent reported to Schoenberg on 14 June, writing: 'We have not found anything for the Zemlinskys yet. I think there is hardly any chance. Alex should look for a flat.'[14] Whilst Mathilde eventually managed to secure the same house that the Schoenbergs stayed in the previous year, *Engelgut*, number 22, the fact that Schoenberg appears to have taken care of his own accommodation without any concern as to his brother-in-law's is an indication that Zemlinsky's relationship with Schoenberg was not in its healthiest state. Mathilde's worried letter to her husband of 17 June tends to suggest as much: 'Are you pleased that the Zemlinskys are coming? How are you getting on with Alex now? . . . They have suffered somewhat with the child.'[15]

The deterioration in relations between Zemlinsky and Schoenberg may have had its roots in December 1907, when Zemlinsky's adaptation of three Dehmel poems of love, betrayal and death, was to be followed within a day or so by Schoenberg, who promptly wrote two lieder based on Stefan George's poems on much the same subject. Whether these competitive compositions were already connected in some way to tensions regarding Mathilde's relationship with Gerstl can only be surmised, but, nonetheless, the rift seems to have continued into their joint summer vacation.

Zemlinsky now managed to fall out with his sister Mathilde too, who complained a few days later that she found Alex 'a bit much,'[16] although, in organising Zemlinsky's accommodation, Mathilde may have eased things between them, as Mathilde's relieved letter infers: 'Alex wrote at last today. If the child is better, they would like to come on Thursday.'[17] However, she was soon upset again by Zemlinsky deliberately ignoring her and perhaps Schoenberg too, as Mathilde angrily reported on 24 June: 'The Zemlinskys are coming tomorrow. I don't think that I want to have much to do with them. I got very upset with Alex. He has written to Mother: "I send you and the children regards" [note: no mention of his sister] I find that this is really not necessary.'[18]

Fig. 7, *Prestgütl*,
Traunstein 24, *c.*1920.
Private collection

Fig. 8, Gerstl's *Zemlinsky* 1.7m
Stiftung Sammlung Kamm,
Kunsthaus Zug

Fig. 9, Zemlinsky, 1.55m (5'1")
ASC

A letter to Alma dated 26 June, the day after he arrived in Gmunden gives some idea of Zemlinsky's black mood, and suggests that he found himself somewhat reluctantly with the Schoenbergs in Gmunden:

This is not yet the letter I owe you, and which I would have liked to write. In the last few weeks I have suffered quite a bit. Our child was seriously ill – it improved somewhat during the last few days, so we packed up and came here. So since yesterday, I am again on the Traunsee – but still not in the mood to write that letter. But I want to thank you sincerely for your invitation. I don't think I will forego it. If I can get away from here, I will come in August.[19]

Unsurprisingly then, Schoenberg travelled alone to Gmunden the next day, arriving, perhaps as a pointed gesture to his wife, a day after Zemlinsky and a day ahead of Gerstl. Schoenberg and Zemlinsky, as good citizens, registered their arrival in the Gmundner Kurliste on 8 July.[20] Gerstl did not, but, arriving on 28 June, took up residence in the same accommodation, the *Feramühle*, that he had stayed in the previous year, and the die for the summer's drama was cast.

Although it would appear from Mathilde's letters to her husband that Schoenberg suspected Mathilde and Gerstl, he nonetheless behaved in a manner that belies his doubts. Indeed, Gerstl appears to have been so welcome within Schoenberg's circle, that he soon went about executing portraits of Schoenberg's family and friends at their lakeside residences, amongst which was Gerstl's *Zemlinsky*.

As can be seen from the absence of his spectacles, Zemlinsky displays a certain vanity in his portrait. However, he may not have yet overcome the misery of his daughter's plight and his unemployed state, for Gerstl portrays him with a serious, even downcast look.

The painting, measuring 1.7 metres, is life size in the true sense (Fig. 8), comparing closely with Zemlinsky's own height of 1.55 metres or about 5' 1" (Fig. 9). Despite the size, Gerstl painted Zemlinsky quickly, much as van Gogh had created his own *plein-air* works. Highlighting his subject with a ghostly halo, Gerstl reveals Zemlinsky as a sepulchral, spiritual figure, the waters of the Traunsee merging with his legs, and the left side of his body dissolving into the background, whilst his left hand is barely a shadow against his pristine white suit jacket.

Gerstl, perhaps for reasons of economy, perhaps for reasons of self-loathing, had used a previously painted canvas, choosing to reverse a self-portrait from around 1904 (Fig. 10), which he had defiled, possibly at a time when, having spent some time in a sanatorium, he may have been suffering certain psychological problems of self-esteem. Having cut the original in two, Gerstl used the other half of this canvas to produce a full-length portrait of Mathilde,[21] presumably at around the same time as that of Zemlinsky, and executed perhaps, as the blades of grass found in the paint at the bottom of the picture might infer, in the gardens of the Schoenbergs' farmhouse.

Zemlinsky's portrait, however, was most probably located on the small bank outside Zemlinsky's summerhouse, number 22 where, the previous year, Schoenberg and Mathilde had been photographed in a series of shots, possibly taken by Zemlinsky himself (Fig. 11). Indeed Gerstl's painting itself has something of the spontaneity of a photograph, which may give some clue as to the circumstances.

Fig. 10, Richard Gerstl *Fragment of a Laughing Self-portrait*, verso of *Alexander Zemlinsky* Stiftung Sammlung Kamm, Kunsthaus Zug

Fig. 11, Arnold & Mathilde Schoenberg on the eastern bank of the Traunsee outside *Engelgut*, Traunstein 22,

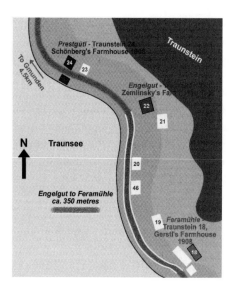

Fig. 12, Map of the eastern bank of the Traunsee, showing the farmhouses inhabited by Schoenberg, Zemlinsky and Gerstl in summer 1908. Design: Oliver Spero, 2007

For example, the map in Fig. 12 shows where the farmhouses, whilst separated by about 400 metres, were situated in relation to each other. It illustrates how Gerstl and the others may have conducted daily life, when it might just be imagined that Gerstl simply bumped into Zemlinsky one morning on the way from the *Feramühle* to Schoenberg's farmhouse, and suggesting a quick portrait, quickly painted his evocative representation.

Certainly Gerstl appears to catch Zemlinsky in the glow of morning since, from the angle of the light, Zemlinsky appears to be facing east, possibly as the sun rose above the Traunstein, to which the glistening waves and Zemlinsky's insistence on a sun hat bear some witness. The walking stick, a legacy from his childhood photo, betrays the adherence to long treks that Schoenberg, and presumably Zemlinsky too, were reputed to have enjoyed and which are described in postcards from Gmunden from the previous year.[22]

There is also a possibility that Zemlinsky may not have had the patience to stay in this possibly impromptu pose for too long, and this may have been one of the reasons for Gerstl's rapid brushwork, although his swirling strokes are typical of others that he completed in 1908. Above all, with its lack of definition in the boundaries between Zemlinsky's human form, the moving water, the solid earth and perhaps even sky, this picture can be seen as painted during a time when Gerstl's expressionist works were at their most potent. Indeed it may simply have been the precursor, or perhaps the successor to another Gerstl painting, which may even have been painted later that same day, for in a depiction of six members of Schoenberg's circle (Fig. 13), again reminiscent of a photographic pose, Zemlinsky is to be seen in the same suit and hat that he wore for his individual portrait. In addition to Zemlinsky and Schoenberg, the group includes Ida and Mathilde, plus an unidentified couple, one of whom may have been one of Schoenberg's students, possibly Karl Horwitz, and his new wife.

Gerstl was known to use a one-metre brush and a spatula in creating his works from Gmunden in 1908, and the extraordinary effect that he attained there can be especially evidenced by his devastation of form, which, whilst avoiding a complete descent into abstraction, brilliantly retains recognition of his subjects. Moreover, although he was almost certainly unacquainted with his contemporaries, Gerstl, in satisfying his subjective vision by deliberately distorting images with thick swirling textured brushstrokes, suggests that he should be considered amongst the very first Austrian, even German, expressionists, and surely before the likes of Kokoschka and Schiele.

As regards their chronology, it is almost certain that these paintings were executed sometime during July 1908, and well before the Gerstl–Mathilde affair was close to its denouement, thus providing some pointers to Zemlinsky's activities during his unemployed break between the two opera houses and his involvement in his sister's affair. One clue can perhaps be found in Zemlinsky's letter to Alma, wherein he appears to have been determined to accept her invitation, probably to visit Toblach in August. It must be said that there is no proof of Zemlinsky's

Fig. 13, *Schönberg group*
Oil on Canvas, 169 x 110 cm
Stiftung Sammlung Kamm, Kunsthaus
Zug

attendance there, although Mahler was certainly entertaining guests, as evidenced by Mahler's invitation to the baritone Anton van Rooy who, in a letter dated 23 August 1908, apologised for his failure to turn up.

It is somewhat intriguing that this dating firmly indicates that Gerstl was painting these sociable paintings, not only whilst he may have been having a liaison with Mathilde, but also at the same time that Schoenberg was writing his seminal Second String Quartet. Here, for the work's innovative 'atonal' fourth movement, Schoenberg adapted George's poem 'Entrueckung', with its famous first line 'I feel air from another planet'. When the sentiment of this poem, together with that of 'Litanei', which Schoenberg used in the third movement, are coupled with the inferences gained from Schoenberg's emancipation of atonality, it is unsurprising that much controversy has evolved over whether Schoenberg was representing the Mathilde–Gerstl affair in this work. Indeed, it has been suggested that, in the second movement, Schoenberg even incorporated musical anagrams equating to the names Mathilde, Gerstl and Schoenberg himself.[23] Flames have been added by Schoenberg's use in the second movement of a musical reference to the Vienna folk song, 'Ach du lieber Augustine', which contains the line 'Alles ist hin,' or 'everything has gone, it's all over,' to which several interpretations have been applied. For example, was Schoenberg, in his use of texts and musical references simply alluding to the end of tonality? Or to the departure of Mahler? Or to the end of his marriage? Or a mixture of all? And could Schoenberg have inspired Gerstl to disintegrate form in his 1908 Gmunden portraits, or was the reverse true?

It also has to be wondered precisely what role Zemlinsky played in his sister's affair, especially in view of his avowed loyalty to her, which may have prevailed over any that he felt for Schoenberg. Zemlinsky's 'voracious appetite for the opposite sex,'[24] and his permissive approach to infidelity might suggest that he would not have stood in Mathilde's way as regards Gerstl. Indeed, suggestions exist that Zemlinsky visited his sister whilst she stayed with Gerstl in his studio after their flight from Gmunden, although this involvement may have indirectly led Webern, who was also close to Zemlinsky, to find her and eventually persuade her to return to Schoenberg. If Zemlinsky had been complicit in Mathilde's affair, this seems to have cast a further pall over his relationship with Schoenberg, even though Schoenberg generally spoke of his first teacher with esteem and affection. Within eighteen months or so, Schoenberg could no longer remain neighbours with Zemlinsky and found new accommodation in Hietzing. Zemlinsky moved a few months later. They continued to holiday together, but a breach occurred in 1912, after which they hardly spoke for a year. The two were never the same again, and the relationship virtually broke down after Mathilde's death in 1923, with Zemlinsky actually choosing to miss his sister's funeral, apparently as a result of his disapproval of an undefined element of Schoenberg's behaviour at the time. There was a brief moment of reconciliation before Zemlinsky's death in 1942, but by then Schoenberg's competitive nature had caused Zemlinsky to pointedly write that, whilst their friendship was once intimate, Schoenberg had emerged the victor.[25]

But out of all this, the most intriguing question is how did a tiny, meek woman such as Mathilde Schoenberg, née Zemlinsky, have such an impact on the artists around her. In addition to Gerstl, who painted her several times, there is evidence that she was represented in several of the most significant compositions of the 20th century. Whilst there are several published and sometimes controversial musicological arguments concerning the representation of Mathilde in various works, it does seem that Mathilde has a case to answer here. For example, not only has it been suggested that, as indicated earlier, Schoenberg utilised motifs for Mathilde and Gerstl in his Second String Quartet, but that he also did so in Op. 15, the *Book of the Hanging Gardens*.[26] Moreover, there is persuasive evidence that *Erwartung* and several of Schoenberg's subsequent works can also be seen as representations of the Gerstl affair. Alternatively, Zemlinsky himself quotes variations of the Mathilde motif, AHDE, in his Second String Quartet,[27] amongst other works, whilst his *Eine florentinische Tragödie* can be said to bear relevance to the Gerstl affair, especially since this depicts a fatal outcome to an adulterous affair, although this may also have reference to Alma's liaison with Walter Gropius in 1910.[28] Finally, as is conclusively proven by Berg's notes from the time, Berg placed a secret palindromic programme at the heart of the second movement of his Chamber Concerto, written at the time of Mathilde's death, which centres on the use of Mathilde's AHDE motto, and which, it has been suggested, alludes to the Gerstl affair.[29] However, here there is some reason to suggest that Berg may have actually been alluding to a later affair that Mathilde may have had in 1920, this time with a young student of Schoenberg, especially as Berg and his wife Helene appear to have been complicit in Mathilde's possible infidelity on this occasion.[30]

Thus, despite the lack of information about Zemlinsky at the time, his portrait helps inform the events of an extraordinary two months in the summer of 1908, when, as a result of his sister's elevation from *frau* to *femme fatale*, twentieth-century art and music may have been transformed for ever.

Notes

1 Beaumont, Antony (2000) *Zemlinsky*. London: Faber and Faber.
   A work that provided essential background information to this article.
2 Email, 21 May 2002
3 Beaumont, 2000, p.165
4 For example, see: Schönberg, Arnold (1921) *Gedanken über Zemlinsky*. Vienna: Arnold Schönberg Center.
5 See: *http://www.museumonline.at/1997/schulen/weiz/index1.htm*
6 See: *http://bilddatenbank.belvedere.at/sammlung.php?obid=4601*

7   See: Arnold Schoenberg Collection, Library of Congress, Washington, DC (ASC/LOC).

8   Postcard from Ida and Alexander Zemlinsky, *c.*25 June 1907, private collection.

9   Kallir, Otto (1974) 'Richard Gerstl (1883–1908), Beiträge zur Dokumentation seines Lebens und Werkes', in *Mitteilungen der Österreichischen Galerie*, 18, 1974, p.117.

10   Breicha, Otto (1993) *Gerstl und Schönberg – Eine Beziehung.* Salzburg: Verlag Galerie Welz, p.22.

11   See: *Paar im Grünen* at http://www.leopoldmuseum.com/index_en.html

12   As per postcard from August Guttmann, Melanie Clark Rice's father, dated 4 August 1907, private collection.

13   Ibid.

14   Mathilde Schönberg to Arnold Schönberg (MS–AS), 14 June 1908, ASC/LOC.

15   MS–AS, 17 June 1908, ASC/LOC

16   MS–AS, 21 June 1908, ASC/LOC

17   MS–AS, 24 June 1908, ASC/LOC

18   MS–AS, 2nd letter, 24 June 1908, ASC/LOC

19   Zemlinsky to Alma Mahler, 26 June 1908, Mahler–Werfel Papers, Rare Book & Manuscript Library, University of Pennsylvania.

20   Gmundner Kurliste, 1908, Kammerhofmuseum, Gmunden.

21   See: *Mathilde Schönberg im Garten* at http://www.leopoldmuseum.com/index_en.html

22   Postcard from Zemlinsky, Schönberg, and others, 30 July 1907, private collection.

23   Dale, Catherine (1993) *Tonality and Structure in Schoenberg's Second String Quartet, Op. 10.* New York & London: Garland Publishing, p.157.

24   Beaumont, 2000, p.27

25   Ibid. pp.407–8

26   Forte, Allen (1978) 'Schoenberg's Creative Evolution: The Path to Atonality', *The Musical Quarterly* 64/2, pp.133–76.

27   Beaumont, 2000, p.234

28   Ibid. p.245

29   Dalen, Brenda (1989) 'Freundschaft, *Liebe, und Welt*': *The Secret Programme of the Chamber Concerto* in *The Berg Companion*, ed. Douglas Jarman. Boston: Northeastern University Press, pp.141–80.

30   Coffer, Raymond (2005) *Soap Opera and Genius in the Second Viennese School, The affairs of Mathilde Schönberg in Alban Berg's Chamber Concerto*, http://igrs.sas.ac.uk/postgraduate/students_pages/raymond_coffer1.htm (cited version), or in *Peabody News*, Johns Hopkins University, March/April, 2005, pp.22–4.

Pamela Tancsik and David Smith

Zemlinsky's Impact on Contemporary Opera During his Stay in Prague Between 1911 and 1927

PRAGUE, TODAY THE CAPITAL of the Czech Republic, had been a city of three cultures – Czech, German and Jewish – for more than 800 years. This came to a violent end only with the occupation by Hitler's troops in 1939. Situated in the heart of Middle Europe, the old Bohemian capital town was also an important centre of music throughout this history. Mozart's *Don Giovanni*, premièred here at the Nostiz Theatre[1] in 1787, was so popular that the melodies were whistled in the streets of Prague by everyone – or so Mozart claimed.

While Prague's population and culture in Mozart's day was predominantly German, this had changed dramatically by the beginning of the twentieth century.

A demographic shift occurred in the second half of the nineteenth century when, through rapid urbanisation, the Czech population in Prague increased from 50,000 in 1858 to 122,000 in 1882, while the German population declined from 73,000 to 37,000.

By 1900, 415,000 Czechs and only 35,000 Germans lived in Prague, which represented a minority of only six per cent of the population. One-third of the German-speaking population was Jewish, many of whom were of course bilingual. After 1882 the Germans no longer held the majority in the Bohemian federal state parliament and the influence of the 'Young Czech' movement in politics worsened the climate of relations between Czechs and Germans. In 1890 the 'Young Czechs' achieved a victory over the 'Old Czech' conservative parties and an exclusivist nationalism rapidly developed on both sides. The nationalism culminated in a language dispute and in 1881 the oldest university in Middle Europe, the Prague Charles University, was divided into a Czech and a German institution. Building a national theatre seemed to be a logical consequence, a fitting symbol of the newborn idea of national identity. With money from the Czech population in Prague, the Czech national theatre, the Národní Divadlo, was established in 1883.

Five years later, on 5 January 1888, the Neues Deutsches Theater, (New German Theatre, hereafter NDT) was ceremonially opened. In a similar way to the Czechs

Fig. 1, Neues
Deutsches Theater
(The New German
Theatre)

the Germans called on support from their community, and so German industrialists
and individual patriots collected the funds to build the theatre.

From the time of its foundation in 1888 the NDT had to withstand strong
competition from the Národní Divadlo. By 1885 Angelo Neumann, the founder and
first director of the German theatre, had managed to obtain the sole performance
rights for the complete works of Richard Wagner.[2] This status began to change when
Neumann and the director of the Czech National Theatre, Šubert, signed a special
'repertoire-contract' which enabled the Národní Divadlo to première all Czech,
French and Italian works while the NDT had the première rights for all works
written within the Austro-Hungarian Empire. Those sole repertoire rights were valid
for three months; after that period the works could be performed in both theatres.
Unfortunately this remained a plan in theory only and did not work in practice.
The idea was prompted by pragmatic and economic considerations that allowed
two theatres to cover the entire repertoire, but it was overruled by the popular
attitude that preferred the theatre of one's own national identity. One could say that
culturally audiences voted with their feet.

Thus, it was as if Germans and Czechs in Prague lived on two different planets:
there was hardly any recognition on the part of either side of the other's culture. One
of the very few exceptions to this attitude was the bilingual Jewish author Max Brod
who commented on the situation of self-imposed apartheid in Prague:

> Prague was a city formed out of two or three cities, the model for its monuments was
> marked by Czech, Jewish and Austrian traditions or even their mixtures, duplications
> and interferences; the pleasure of the one group was the horror of the other and what
> the one group praised as justice and satisfaction meant for the other one injustice
> and revenge.[3]

After Angelo Neumann's death in 1910 the dramaturge and journalist Heinrich Teweles became director of the NDT. It was Teweles who appointed Alexander Zemlinsky as chief conductor of the NDT in 1911.

Prague in 1911 was still part of the Austro-Hungarian Empire. According to Zemlinsky the number of regular theatre-goers was no higher than 600 on average. The NDT repertoire at the time consisted mainly of opera, operetta, a small amount of ballet and regular Philharmonic concerts.

Zemlinsky himself conducted about one-third of the opera repertoire, about forty performances per season. He focused mainly on the German repertoire, operas by Wagner, Strauss and Mozart. Since he was in the position to choose his repertoire, it is interesting to note that the only Italian operas he ever conducted at the NDT were Verdi's *Aida* and Puccini's *Trittico (Il Tabarro, Suor Angelica* and *Gianni Schicchi)*. He was otherwise not interested in conducting Italian operas and delegated that task to his colleagues at the NDT.

Zemlinsky's stay in Prague lasted for fifteen years. One assumes that he enjoyed his stay: why otherwise would he decide to stay on for such a long time? The opposite is, in fact, closer to the truth. Zemlinsky tried more than once to land a position elsewhere. To him Prague was a cultural backwater; furthermore he had to put up with his theatre director's ignorance of his work as a composer. Why then did Zemlinsky accept this position in a provincial town like Prague in the first place?

Fig. 2, Alexander Zemlinsky in Prague

Fig. 3, Heinrich Teweles, Director of the NDT from 1911 to 1918

Gustav Mahler's death on 18 May 1911 was a great loss to the world; but it was in particular a blow for his admirers and friends. One of them was Zemlinsky who lost in Gustav Mahler his one and only mentor. It was Mahler who had made possible the first performance of Zemlinsky's second opera, *Es war einmal,* at the Wiener Hofoper in 1900 and it was he who had wanted Zemlinsky as a conductor at the Hofoper seven years later. Mahler had also planned the première of Zemlinsky's third opera, *Der Traumgörge.* Zemlinsky's lucky streak came to an abrupt end after Mahler's resignation from the Hofoper in the autumn of 1907. Mahler's successor, Felix von Weingartner, did not keep his promise and the première of *Der Traumgörge* was cancelled and so also was Zemlinsky's employment. In the end Zemlinsky got nowhere in Vienna and so it is not such a surprise that he accepted the opportunity in Prague. Of course, for him Prague was never meant to be a long-term residence, but things changed with the outbreak of World War One in 1914.

Zemlinsky's early years in Prague were overshadowed by the constraints of the war. Many members of the company and the orchestra were conscripted. Everything and everyone – musicians, singers, food, material and labour – was limited. There was a constant shortage of coal to heat the theatre, a lack of candles to illuminate it and of course no food for casts or staff either. There were not enough materials such as wood, paint or canvas for set-building. Not only did an ailing economy make theatre work difficult but war propaganda also dictated the repertoire of the country's theatres. For example, several popular operas composed by living composers who belonged to the nations fighting against Germany – such as the works of Puccini, Mascagni and Leoncavallo – were banned. Despite this measure, *La Bohème* continued to be performed at the NDT throughout the war.

Zemlinsky did not fear controversy or criticism but he was disappointed that Prague as a centre of music was not more highly thought-of in the wider world. Only a few music-lovers who came especially to Prague saw his quality of work. As early as 1914 Zemlinsky felt frustrated and wanted to leave the Bohemian capital. When he told Schoenberg about it, he got this reply:

> ...What is the matter? Why don't you want to stay on in Prague? At least until you find the position you deserve. This can't go on forever. But you have to look at Prague as if it were for a short while only. I think since you arrived you have made something different out of it. And even if Prague was seen only as a stopover point, it has become something since your arrival, and this must find acknowledgement soon. I certainly will not say that you should stay in Prague. No – you should go away but only because there are places with more and better opportunities. But this is only one of two reasons [for staying] (the second one is the already existing reputation of a famous old theatre). But everything else depends on you and you have restored its reputation!! And after all, you have a self-created position in which you can stay on for as long as it takes. I can understand your impatience. Your director

is an idiot, the audience is small and right now there is hardly any feedback from abroad. I understand that you want to perform the works as they ought to be. But you would be very surprised if you knew how bad the work is at famous theatres. I'm quite sure that you would get your way, but the audience does not seem to react to differences in quality. And that is why it is of no consequence where you are; it only counts when you can work properly.[4]

Schoenberg's warning must have had an effect because Zemlinsky stayed on despite the difficult circumstances. Furthermore, he managed to realise most of his plans. Through his leadership the following contemporary works found their way on to the stage of the NDT during the war: the melodrama *Enoch Arden* by Richard Strauss in 1915; one year later, Max von Schilling's *Mona Lisa*; and an one-act opera by Zemlinsky's pupil, Erich Wolfgang Korngold, *Der Ring des Polykrates*, based on a libretto by director Heinrich Teweles, was first performed in November 1916.

Franz Schreker's *Der Ferne Klang*, planned for 1916, could only be realised in 1920. Finally on 4 March 1917, one of Zemlinsky's own works, his one-act opera *Eine florentinische Tragödie*, based on the play by Oscar Wilde, was produced. It was given together with Julius Bittner's singspiel *Das Höllisch Gold*. The music critic Felix Adler, writing in the German newspaper Bohemia, described Zemlinsky's composition as having a very strong and immediate effect on the audience. He described the music as euphonious, and full of warmth and 'inwardness'.[5]

In Zemlinsky's attempts to attract audiences to the NDT, the war situation was not the only challenge for him. With the independence of the newly formed Czechoslovakian state after World War One in 1918, the political and economic situation worsened for the small German community in Prague. The new director of the NDT, the Prague-born actor Leopold Kramer faced a difficult situation. He was now director of a minority theatre in the new Czechoslovakian state where, from 1920, Czech was the only official language.

Fig. 4, Director of the
NDT from 1918 to 1927,
Leopold Kramer

A bigger difference between the actor-director Leopold Kramer and Zemlinsky is hard to imagine. Kramer, described as a handsome, tall and charming performer, was most convincing on stage in the contemporary drama style of Naturalism, as demonstrated in plays by Hermann Bahr, Arthur Schnitzler, Anton Wildgans and Karl Schönherr. His versatile talent enabled him to succeed in comedies and classical dramas as well. Kramer was outgoing, confident and apparently not educated or even interested in music. Zemlinsky's talent as a composer was obviously overlooked by Kramer. In a letter to Kramer in 1920 in which Zemlinsky asks for leave while composing his opera *Der Zwerg*, he refers to Kramer's lack of understanding of his music:

> Here, on the one hand, I have absolute tranquillity and time, but on the other hand, I convince myself that I can count on your understanding even though you don't know me as a composer, never mind being able to value me. ... All the prepared work is delegated and disposed and you mustn't fear any mishaps in the development of repertoire caused through my absence. ... But I promise – and can do that today with an easy conscience – that my opera will sound good. I'm only afraid this may be a matter of indifference to you, however....[6]

The relationship between Kramer and Zemlinsky went through several stages of crisis. Kramer's position as the director of a minority theatre was not easy. The NDT in the young Czech Republic had to function with a much smaller subsidy than most other opera houses of the same size in Germany and Austria at the time. In 1925 Kramer commented on this issue in a newspaper article: '...The director has to make concessions to his audience's taste and as long as he does that, without harming the artistic quality of his theatre, nobody can object. This was the case at all times. ... Here in Prague the circumstances are probably even more difficult, because the theatre operates on a "small island" populated by Germans.'[7]

Zemlinsky did not believe in politics but he believed in the power of music. When the repertoire contract expired in the late 1920s, Zemlinsky took the opportunity to introduce the German minority in Prague to several Czech operas. He also appeared as the first Austrian conductor to lead the Czech Philharmonic Orchestra.

All this happened while the tension between the two nations in the newly formed republic increased. The climax of the crisis was the violent expropriation of the *Deutsches Landestheater* on 18 November 1920. This led to the loss of the second theatre for the German community in Prague.

The Czech government promised to provide another venue but this never materialised. The claim for compensation was finally settled after a court judgment in February 1921 and gave the German community only a financial compensation. With the loss of the second venue for the German Theatre, the drama section had to be closed for a while, which resulted in a big deficit. This plunged the NDT into huge debts until 1923.

It was through Zemlinsky's extraordinary efforts that the NDT could impress its audience with a number of exceptional performances, which also won admiration outside of Prague.

On 4 January 1921, Zemlinsky had completed his opera *Der Zwerg*, that he had started only the previous year on June 20 in Prague. His hope of having the new work performed in Vienna was not fulfilled but his ex-colleague Otto Klemperer, who later became music director at the Cologne Opera House, offered to present the world première there and Zemlinsky accepted. It was a major success. The critic in the *Kölnische Zeitung* wrote '[H]e is as much a master of technique and form in small details as in larger scenes...' and the *Kölnische Volkszeitung* praised Zemlinsky's opera: '...in terms of artistic refinement the opera has surpassed almost every modern work that in recent years has graced the Cologne stage.'[8]

On 3 March 1923 three one-act-operas by Paul Hindemith were performed at the NDT: *Mörder, Hoffnung der Frauen; Sancta Susanna* and *Das Nusch-Nuschi*. The Russian tenor and stage director Louis Laber directed the triptych. Costumes and sets were based on Mikhail Andreenko's constructivist designs. Andreenko, like Louis Laber born in Ukraine, belonged to the art movement of constructivists under the leadership of El Lissitzky. Like many other progressive artists he left Russia in 1923, worked as a set-designer in Europe and settled in Paris where he died in 1982. He had also designed theatre sets for the Národní Divadlo in 1924.

The Prague production of the Hindemith triple-bill was the first one to be mounted after the two scandal-provoking performances in Stuttgart and Frankfurt, where the operas had been premièred in 1921 and 1922. The most controversial work was *Sancta Susanna*, written by the expressionistic 'Staccato-poet' August Stramm, who had died in 1915, in World War One, at the age of 41.

The story of *Sancta Susanna* is set in a convent. Two nuns, Susanna and Klementia, witness a girl in front of the crucifix at the altar, who confesses that she has had intercourse with her lover. When the lover suddenly appears, Sister Klementia remembers an event she once witnessed: a young nun pressing her naked body against a crucifix. The nun was punished by being entombed alive in a wall. Susanna, who is inspired by the story, takes off her clothes and walks towards the crucifix. Klementia cannot stop Susanna and when the other nuns arrive and see her, they curse her as a devil.

Unlike in Frankfurt and Stuttgart the Hindemith operas did not cause any scandal in Prague, and Zemlinsky in particular was praised for his excellent and vigorous interpretation. The Prague critics were undecided about *Das Nusch-Nuschi* and *Mörder, Hoffnung der Frauen*, but their praise assured the success of *Sancta Susanna*.

Zemlinsky was not only the chief conductor of the NDT. His workload in Prague was enormous; like Gustav Mahler, he had only the summer holidays in which to work on his own compositions. As opera director he had to conduct approximately six performances per month. He believed in extensive rehearsals and always aimed for the highest quality. In 1922 he also became president of the newly formed Prager Verein für Musikalische Privataufführungen. For the opening in May 1922, Schoenberg's *Pierrot lunaire* was performed. During its short existence until 1924, the Verein presented altogether fifty-six compositions in fourteen concerts, mostly works by Reger, Debussy, Schoenberg, Berg and Webern.

Fig. 5, Poster advertising the world première of Erwartung

The first international acknowledgment for Zemlinsky came in 1924 with the *Festival of the International Society for Contemporary Music*, the ISCM Festival,[9] which was presented in Prague for the first time. Part of the festival programme which was attended by Czech President Tomás Garrique Masaryk was the world première of Schoenberg's monodrama *Erwartung*. Marie Gutheil-Schoder performed the solo part of the woman ('Die Frau').

Schoenberg's new work should have been performed in Prague the previous year but Zemlinsky had to postpone it. The thirty-minute-long expressionistic monologue was mainly composed using voice-leading by semitone intervals. Zemlinsky's friend, the poet and dermatologist Marie Pappenheim, was the librettist. Even Schoenberg did not have the audacity to première the work in Vienna, where it might have caused another scandal. To him Prague was the right place, with an audience far less conservative than the Viennese one.

Erwartung is a monologue resembling the speeded-up visions of a feverish dream.[10] A woman, simply called 'Die Frau', walks through a dark forest in search of her lover. In the end she discovers his dead body. As she looks into his staring eyes she finds 'a memory of his suspected infidelity'.[11]

The composition does not contain any repeated musical material and none of the themes and motifs used is related to any other. The performance was a great success for Schoenberg but would have been impossible without Zemlinsky. The Prague critic Ernst Rychnovsky wrote: 'Zemlinsky achieved, with the performance of Schoenberg's piece which was considered unperformable, an artistic act that has to be listed in future opera history as a turning point. The audience by simply listening can't imagine all the difficulties of this music, which constitutes in performance an eternal flow. The audience cannot appreciate how Zemlinsky had to rehearse each bar over and over again to get the result of something which sounds as easy as a children's game.'[12]

Despite this triumph the relationship between Zemlinsky and his director Kramer was heading for a major crisis. In July 1924, from his summer holiday destination Alt-Aussee, Zemlinsky sent the following accusatory lines to Kramer:

> ...You can blame me for being trivial but I have to start with a terrible lament about Life! Summer! Money! Soon everything will be over without my having had a recovery at all. It is terrible. But when I get more horrible news about the opera programme, such as *Queen of Saba*, *Ariadne* and the *Bildnis der Madonna* by Marcer Frickel, then I am in complete despair. This must be a bad joke? I do know Mr. Frickel (second violinist of the Wiener Volksoper),[13] a dilettante, who creates the worst possible kitsch ... But believe me, if you want to produce something new, then you must do such things as can give the theatre new values and a new attitude. Besides, one is forced to produce kitsch in any case.[14]

Zemlinsky was tired of Prague but nevertheless he continued to support performances of contemporary operas at the NDT. On 21 April 1925 he conducted Alban Berg's *Wozzeck Fragments*, or – better put – three scenes out of the fifteen of his opera *Wozzeck*.

The fragments consisted of three monologues: the third scene of Act I (Marie's lullaby for her child), the first scene of Act III (Marie's feelings of guilt at being unfaithful to Wozzeck), and the final scene of Act III (where Marie's child learns of her mother's death). The fragments were a success and in particular Zemlinsky's vigorous and energetic performance indicated that a première of the whole piece would follow quite soon.

It then came down to a real competition between Zemlinsky and Otokar Ostrčil, director of the Czech National Theatre, as to who would get the full performance rights. Due to director Kramer's hesitating attitude and the financial situation of the NDT, the Národní Divadlo finally prevailed.

Yet the battle was not won entirely by the Czech National Theatre. The *Wozzeck* première caused the cancellation of the scheduled performance of the Czech opera *Dědův odkaz (The Legacy of the Grandfather)* by Vitězlav Novàk. The composer protested and this led to a major scandal during the performance of the opera at the Národní Divadlo. In Prague's theatre history this is known as the '*Wozzeck Affair*'. Alban Berg's new work had caused a major political crisis between German and Czech nationalists.

Despite all this, Zemlinsky fearlessly conducted Czech operas at the NDT for the German community. His first successful attempt had been the production of Smetana's *Der Kuss* (*Hubička*) in German on 20 March 1924. Nothing proves more clearly the long-standing hostility between Czechs and Germans in Prague than the fact that this Czech opera was only performed before a German audience in 1924, forty-eight years after the première in Prague. Similarly Smetana's *Die Verkaufte Braut* had to wait for nearly sixty years from the time of its première before it was played before the German audience in Prague.

While Smetana's works already belonged to the classic repertoire, the performance of Leoš Janáček's *Jenufa* on 23 October 1926 at the NDT was a far more ambitious attempt to expose the German audience to contemporary Czech music. Janáček's opera was first performed in 1904 in Brno but came to Prague only in 1916.

The composer, unlike Smetana, was still alive, though one could say that at more than seventy years of age only just alive. Max Brod, who translated the Czech novel by Gabriele Preiß into German, has to be thanked for making the production at the NDT possible. The critic praised Zemlinsky's unselfish artistic approach and his minute attention to detail in his care for Janáček's composition.

Rychnovsky's review claimed that 'even Janáček could hardly have wished to hear this or that differently'.[15] It was an extraordinary success and the first curtain-calls began after the first act.

Fig. 6, Set design
by Emil Pirchan for
Jenufa at the NDT
(1926)

In the season 1926–7 the crisis at the NDT was obvious. While before 1918 the proportion of operas to operettas was two-thirds to one-third, now in 1927 three times more operettas were given than operas. Furthermore the Philharmonic Concerts had to be cancelled due to the lack of audience.

In the late 1920s Zemlinsky conducted fewer performances than before 1918, but he still impressed the audience with a number of exceptional interpretations of contemporary works. Yet, it was noticeable that Zemlinsky increasingly lost interest in his work in Prague, disliking Leopold Kramer's repertoire plans. Despite the latter's focus on operettas and light-hearted works, Zemlinsky managed to present three other contemporary works besides *Jenufa*, as follows: on 19 February 1927, *Der wunderbare Mandarin* by Bèla Bartók; on 13 March 1927, Hindemith's new opera *Cardillac*; and, as his last première, Ernst Krenek's 'hit', *Jonny spielt auf* on 16 June 1927.

After Cologne, the NDT was the second stage in the world to perform Bartók's ballet. The NDT was also progressive in the case of Hindemith, it being the fourth theatre after Dresden, Wiesbaden and Vienna to stage *Cardillac*. Krenek's jazz-opera, *Jonny spielt auf*, was Zemlinsky's last achievement in contemporary opera before he left Prague.

Zemlinsky was admired as a conductor by his far more famous colleagues, for example, Igor Stravinsky: 'I do believe that, of all the conductors I've ever heard, I would nominate Zemlinsky as the one who consistently maintained the highest level of musical quality in performance. I remember one performance of *Figaros Hochzeit* in Prague as the most satisfactory performance I've ever heard in my life.'[16]

Unlike his colleagues Leo Blech, Otto Klemperer, Erich Kleiber, Bruno Walter or Erwin Pollak who were all appointed to the position of *Generalmusikdirektor*, Zemlinsky never gained such an internationally recognised position. Only in 1927 at the age of fifty-six did he manage to move to the progressive Kroll Opera in the metropolis of Berlin, but luck was never with Zemlinsky for long: the Kroll Opera was forced to close down in July 1931.

If Zemlinsky's ability as a conductor was so highly praised in his time, why did he not achieve lasting fame? And why has the recognition of his own music been so slow in coming?

The music aesthetician Theodor Adorno claimed that Zemlinsky's personality was responsible for this anomaly. In 1963 Adorno wrote: 'In certain circumstances a man may be cheated of his deserts by nothing more than a lack of ruthlessness. It is possible to be too refined for one's own genius, and in the last analysis the greatest talents require a fund of barbarism, however deeply buried.' [17]

This fatal combination of a subtle personality and a lack of ruthlessness may underlie Zemlinsky's absence of ambition in getting his own works produced in Prague. During his stay at the NDT only three of his own compositions had been premièred there: the *Maeterlinck-Gesänge* in 1921, the third version of his opera *Kleider machen Leute* in 1922, and finally the *Lyric Symphony* in 1924. Neither his

Fig. 7, Zemlinsky conducting a rehearsal at the NDT

opera *Eine florentinische Tragödie* nor his opera *Der Zwerg* was staged in Prague during his tenure. On the contrary, he took a different approach in promoting the new works of his composer colleagues Korngold, Hindemith, Schoenberg, Richard Strauss, Schreker, Berg and Krenek.

It is an unusual case in music history that Zemlinsky, who gained so much recognition and respect as a conductor during his lifetime, has never reached the ranks of well-known conductors. In respect of his compositions, it is no different. Despite the fact that all Zemlinsky's operas have now been performed and recorded, his acceptance is still limited to critical acclaim.

Why does a broader recognition of his genius remain a mirage?

List of contemporary operas and Czech operas performed at the NDT between 1911 and 1927

(All premières except *Die heilige Ente, Das Mahl der Spötter* and *Der wunderbare Mandarin* were conducted by Zemlinsky.)

Date	Opera	Composer	World première
19-10-1912	*Es war einmal*	Alexander Zemlinsky	22-01-1900 Vienna
07-12-1912	*Ariadne auf Naxos*	Richard Strauss	25-10-1912 Stuttgart (first version)
01-01-1916	*Mona Lisa*	Max von Schillings	26-09-1915 Stuttgart
17-09-1916	*Kain und Abel*	Felix v. Weingartner	17-05-1914 Darmstadt
16-11-1916	*Der Ring d. Polykrates*	Erich W. Korngold	28-03-1916 Munich
16-11-1916	*Violanta*	Erich W. Korngold	28-03-1916 Munich
01-01-1917	*Ariadne auf Naxos*	Richard Strauss	04-10-1916 Vienna (new version)
04-03-1917	*Eine florentinische Tragödie*	Alexander Zemlinsky	30-01-1917 Stuttgart
07-09-1918	*Die toten Augen*	Eugen d'Albert	05-03-1916 Dresden
20-05-1920	*Der ferne Klang*	Franz Schreker	18-08-1912 Frankfurt
03-12-1921	*Elektra*	Richard Strauss	25-01-1909 Dresden
04-02-1922	*Die tote Stadt*	Erich W. Korngold	04-12-1920 Hamburg
22-04-1922	*Kleider machen Leute*	Alexander Zemlinsky	(première of new version)
30-11-1922	*Ritter Blaubart*	Emil N. von Reznicek	29-01-1920 Darmstadt
03-03-1923	Three One-Act Operas:		
	Mörder, Hoffnung der Frauen	Paul Hindemith	04-06-1921 Stuttgart
	Sancta Susanna	Paul Hindemith	26-03-1922 Frankfurt
	Das Nusch-Nuschi	Paul Hindemith	04-06-1921 Stuttgart
02-02-1924	*Der Schatzgräber*	Franz Schreker	21-01-1920 Frankfurt
20-03-1924	*Der Kuß*	Bedřich Smetana	07-11-1876 Prague
06-06-1924	*Erwartung*	Arnold Schoenberg	World première
05-03-1925	*Intermezzo*	Richard Strauss	04-11-1924 Dresden

19-04-1925	*Wozzeck* (3 Fragments) (première of opera)	Alban Berg	11-06-1924 Frankfurt 14-12-1925 Berlin
	(Première of opera in Czech on 11-11-1926 at Národní Divadlo)		
20-05-1925	*Ariane und Blaubart*	Paul Dukas	10-05-1907 Paris
28-10-1925	*Die Verkaufte Braut*	Bedřich Smetana	30-05-1866 Prague
26-01-1926	*Die heilige Ente*	Hans Gàl	29-04-1923 Düsseldorf
16-02-1926	*Das Mahl der Spötter* (*La Cena delle beffe*)	Umberto Giordano	20-12-1924 Milan
24-02-1926	*König David* (*Le Roi David*)	Arthur Honegger	11-06-1921 Mézières
28-05-1926	*Der Zwerg*	Alexander Zemlinsky	28-05-1922 Cologne
23-10-1926	*Jenufa*	Leoš Janáček	21-01-1904 Brno
19-02-1927	*Der wunderbare Mandarin*	Béla Bartók	28-11-1926 Köln
	Der Schleier der Pierrette	Ernst v. Dohnányi	1910 Dresden
13-03-1927	*Cardillac*	Paul Hindemith	09-11-1926 Dresden
16-06-1927	*Jonny spielt auf*	Ernst Krenek	10-02-1927 Leipzig

Notes

1   The Nostiz Theatre, named after Count Anton Nostiz, was later called Stavovské Divadlo (Stände Theater).

2   Neumann produced in 1878 in Leipzig the first performance of Wagner's *Ring des Nibelungen* outside of Bayreuth. He acquired from Wagner personally the sole performance rights of the 'Ring' until 1887.

3   Max Brod (1966) Der Prager Kreis, Stuttgart: Surhkamp-Taschenbuch Wissenschaft.
    „Prag war eine Stadt aus zwei oder drei Städten, das Muster ihrer Monumente war geprägt von tschechischen, jüdischen und österreichischen Traditionen oder gar ihren Mischungen, Doppelungen und Interferenzen; das Glück der einen war der Schrecken der anderen, und was die einen als Recht und Erfüllung rühmten, war den anderen Entrechtung und Rache".

4   *„...Was ist denn los?Warum willst du denn nicht in Prag bleiben? Wenigstens so lange, bis sich die Stellung findet, die Dir gebührt. Schließlich: Das kann ja doch nicht mehr so lange dauern. Aber mußt du denn Prag so ansehen, als ob es unbedingt nur für den Moment wäre. Ich finde: Seit du dort bist, hast du ja etwas anderes daraus gemacht. Und wenn selbst Prag früher nur als eine ‚Zwischenstation' angesehen werden konnte, ist es doch seit du dort bist, etwas worden, was unbedingt in kurzer Zeit beachtet werden muß! Ich will damit gewiß nicht sagen, daß du in Prag bleiben solltest. Nein, du solltest fort, aber nur: weil es Orte gibt die mehr und bessere Mittel besitzen. Aber das ist auch der eine von bloß 2 Gründen, die es gibt (der Zweite ist: ds schon vorhandene Ansehen eines ‚altberühmten' Theaters). Aber alles andere, hing von Dir ab und du hast es ja zur Höhe gebracht!! Und hast somit immerhin eine (wenn auch von Dir geschaffene) Stelle an der du die kurze Zeit, die es noch dauern kann, ausharren kannst. Ich begreife Deine Ungeduld: Dein Direktor ist ein Esel, das Publikum ist klein un die Wirkung aufs Ausland einstweilen gering. Ich*

begreife, daß du endlich die Sachen so aufführen willst, wie sie gehören. Aber du würdest sehr staunen, wenn du erführst, wie schlecht in berühmten Theatern gearbeitet wird. Ich bin ja sicher, daß du dir anderes durchsetzen würdest, aber das Publikum scheint gar nicht auf Qualitätsunterschiede zu reagieren. Und insofern ist es fast gleichgültig, wo man ist, wenn man nur anständig arbeiten kann." Zemlinsky's Briefwechsel mit Schönberg... (1995) edited by Horst Weber, Darmstadt: Wissenshaftliche Buchgesellschaft.

5   *„...Das Publikum stand ganz im Banne dieser durch ihre klangliche Schönheit und warme Innerlichkeit passenden Musik."* In Pamela Tancsik (2000) Die Prager Oper heißt Zemlinsky, Wein: Böhlau, p.452.

6   *„... Hier habe ich nun absolute Ruhe und Zeit einerseits, andererseits sagte ich mir, daß ich auf ihr Verstehen – wenngleich Sie mich als Komponist gar nicht kennen, geschweige denn schätzen können – sicherlich rechnen kann. ...Es ist alle vorbereitende Arbeit verteilt u. disponiert und es dürfte zunächst durch mein Fernbleiben kein Malheur der Repertoireentwicklung zu befürchten sein. .. Ich verspreche und kann das heute schon mit gutem Gewissen tun, daß die Oper gut klinken [sic] wird. Aber das dürfte Ihnen so ziemlich gleichgültig sein."* Zemlinsky's letter to Kramer (undated), Summer 1920, in Pamela Tancsik (2000) Die Prager Oper heißt Zemlinsky, p.126.

7   *„Der Direktor muß Konzessionen an den Geschmack des Publikums machen und solange er dies tut, ohne das künstlerische Niveau seiner Bühnen zu verletzen, kann man nichts dagegen einwenden. Dies war zu allen Zeiten so. (...) Hier in Prag liegen die Verhältnisse womöglich noch schwieriger, weil das Theater auf einer kleinen von Deutschen bevölkerten Insel steht."* Leopold Kramer (25 December 1925) in *Bohemia*, „Die Zukunft des Sudetendeutschen Theaters", in Pamela Tancsik (2000) Die Prager Oper heißt Zemlinsky, p.127.

8   Antony Beaumont (2000) *Zemlinsky*. Ithaca, New York: Cornell University Press and also London: Faber and Faber, p.311.

9   The ISCM Festival was founded by the British musicologist Edward Dent in Salzburg and took place every year in a different town.

10   Based on a review by HH Stuckenschmidt (1951) Arnold Schönberg, sec. Edition. Zurich and Freiburg: Atlantis Verlag.

11   Stephen Walsh (2001) s.v 'Schoenberg' in *The New Penguin Opera Guide*, ed. Amanda Holden. London: Penguin, p.827.

12   *„Zemlinsky hat mit der Einstudierung dieser bisher auch von Schönberg für unaufführbar gehaltenen Werkes eine künstlerische Tat vollbracht, die in einer künftigen Geschichte der Oper als markant wird verzeichnet werden müssen. Das Publikum macht sich keine rechte Vorstellung von den Schwierigkeiten dieser ...Musik, die sich in ewigem Fluß befindet, und ahnt nicht, welche mühseligen Proben jedes einzelnen Taktes Zemlinsky halten mußte, ehe eine Aufführung zustande kam, die klang, als wäre das, was das Orchester leistete, ein Kinderspiel."* In Pamela Tancsik (2000) Die Prager Oper heißt Zemlinsky, p. 562.

13   Here Zemlinsky was wrong: the composer's name was Marco Fränkl and he played the viola, not the violin. He later changed his name to Marcus Frank.

14   *„… ich beginne auch auf die Gefahr hin trivial zu sein – mit einem schrecklichen*
     Wehgeschrei über das Leben! Sommer, Geld alles wird bald vorüber sein ohne, daß man zu
     wirklicher Erholung kam. Es ist furchtbar. Kommen dann aber noch Schreckensnachrichten
     über den Spielplan der Oper nach welcher ‚Königin von Saba', Ariadne und ‚Das Bildnis
     der Madonna' von Marcer Frickel – also zwei (!) Neueinstudierungen und einer Novität,
     u.z. was für eine! vorgesehen sind, dann verzweifelt man vollends. Das kann doch
     hoffentlich nur ein schlechter Witz sein? Ich kenne Herrn Marcer Frickel (2. Geiger der
     Volksoper) ein Dilettant, der schlechtesten Kitsch aus Kitsch zusammenstellt. … Aber
     glauben Sie mir wenn man neustudieren will, dann gleich solche, die dem Theater einen
     Nimbus der fortschrittlichen Gesinnung geben. Daneben gibt man ohnehin gezwungen
     genug Kitsch." Zemlinsky's letter to Kramer (Summer 1925) in Pamela Tancsik (2000) Die
     Prager Oper heißt Zemlinsky, p.132.

15   Ernst Rychnovsky (24 October 1926) Prager Tagblatt, Prague. *„…Nach einer mit*
     minutiöser Sorgfalt geleiteten Einstudierung gah er an der Oper alles, worauf sie ein
     gutes Recht hatte. Er gab es mit so selbstloser, vom echt künstlerischen Gestus diktierten
     Hingabe, daß Janacek kaum den Wunsch gehabt haben wird dies oder jenes anders zu
     hören.…"

16   *„Ich glaube, daß von all den Dirigenten, die ich gehört habe, ich Zemlinsky als den*
     Dirigenten nominieren würde, der die besten durchweg hohen musikalischen Maßstäbe
     einhielt. Ich erinnere mich einer Aufführung von ‚Figaros Hochzeit' in Prag, als der
     zufriedenstellendsten Opernaufführung, die ich je gehört habe." In Hans Heinsheimer
     (1981) Meine Erinnerungen an Zemlinsky (Programme of the Hamburg State Opera).
     Also Stravinsky (1968/1972) *Themes and Conclusions*. London: Faber and Faber. And see
     Philip Weller's comments on pages 44/5.

17   *„Unter Umständen betrügt ihn nichts anderes um seinen Rang als Mangel an*
     Rücksichtslosigkeitk; einer kann gewissermaßen für die eigene Genialität zu fein sein, und
     am Ende bedürfen die größten Begabungen eines versteckten Fonds an Barbarischen."
     Adorno, TW (1997) ‚Zemlinsky', Quasi una fantasia, *Musicalische Schriften*, ed. Rolf
     Tiedemann, 20 vols. Frankfurt am Main: Suhrkamp Verlag, vol. 16, p.155 (originally
     1963). The translation given here is by Rodney Livingstone (1994) in *Quasi una Fantasia*.
     London and New York: Verso, p.127.

Philip Weller

Ways of the New: Zemlinsky in the Light of History

ADORNO'S 1959 ESSAY ON Zemlinsky, together with the one on Schreker written earlier that same year, was like a flare in the night sky. For all their typically dense and intricate modes of argumentation and their demanding, tough-minded character, this pair of essays briefly illumined the darkness which in the post-war era had enveloped the work of these two exceptionally gifted and accomplished musicians, whose careers had been so closely bound up with the fortunes of the musical culture that was broken, and partly swept away, by the war. Yet what is most immediately striking about the two essays is not so much the difficult question of their lasting insights and their particular combination of virtues and shortcomings (things which will rightly continue to be debated), as the fact that they should exist at all. Why might they both have come into being in the same year? And why these two in particular? What was it that brought them to the surface of Adorno's conscious mind, and drove him to articulate his perhaps inchoate thoughts in the way he did? Finding a possible answer, or range of answers, to these questions will take us inside some of the ambiguities, as well as the discoverable realities, of the Zemlinsky case.[1]

In the first place, it might surprise us to find Adorno talking quite so positively about two composers who, in whatever direction their own musical growth and experimentation may have gone, never followed the path to atonality. Not to have done so was in a sense, viewed in the strictest terms, to have failed to perceive in full measure the musical and cultural realities of that era, in the decades before and after the First World War, for what they were – or perhaps better, to have failed to draw the final artistic consequences from them. The strict and radical view (as seen in retrospect at least) was the one which, taking in social and political as well as purely artistic factors, saw the creative use of dissonance, freely deployed within an atonal framework, as the only viable solution. This was the 'strong' way out of what was perceived as a state of impasse and crisis. Such a development – towards a language of total chromaticism, within a context of expressionistic atonality – had the character of an imperative, grounded in a no doubt simplistic and narrow-minded view of historical necessity, in the mind of Schoenberg. And this dramatic, at times also self-dramatising stance was shared, albeit in differing ways and degrees, by Berg, Webern, Wellesz, Réti and others (including instrumentalists such as Steuermann, Rosé and, later on, Kolisch) who were part of the Schoenbergian radical group. Neither Schreker nor Zemlinsky took this extreme view. Thus Adorno's intellectual commitment to the idea of a strong musical manifestation of 'progressive' or 'advancement' modernism (*Fortschrittsmoderne*), as embodied in the work of Schoenberg and his circle, might well be thought to have precluded so generous an appreciation of their work.

Yet the very existence of the two essays demonstrates clearly that he felt the need nevertheless to come to a balanced assessment of what their work had contributed, not just in individual and aesthetic but in historical, evolutionary terms. And we should note right away that there is a sense in which his revaluation of the contributions of Zemlinsky and Schreker came quite clearly at the expense of Strauss. For while he may have perceived the broader, more circumstantial significance of Strauss as a historical figure – and even more importantly perhaps, in the present context, that of Brahms, about whom he nevertheless wrote relatively little – Adorno was strongly and indeed philosophically resistant to Strauss's music.[2] Viewed in this light, we can begin to understand why he might have set out to find distinctive and characteristic qualities that sounded, and could be heard to sound, in Zemlinsky's and Schreker's music as signs of real intellectual and expressive strength, to highlight these qualities and to argue in their favour as specifically and vividly as he could, for an audience of a new generation.

For despite his tough dialectical understanding of the nature and agency of social and cultural change, Adorno's view of musical modernity and its processes was in the end quite large and flexible enough to encompass them both. And I shall suggest here, at the outset, three reasons why I think this should have been so. First, Adorno was himself caught up in the very process of cultural and artistic development he was observing and trying to account for. He viewed it from a distance and took (as we would expect) a determinedly critical stance, yet was not, and could not be, in any sense disinterested or uninvolved. He knew that he had occupied – and continued to occupy – a privileged and very definite position, given his background and education and, more than anything else, his studies with Berg from January 1925.[3] (We should surely accept the idea that something profound, and profoundly formative, in his notion of Zemlinsky's true worth must have come to him from that source since it was Berg who had, if anybody did, a sympathetic and balanced understanding of the whole Zemlinsky phenomenon.)Adorno's position brought with it obligations as well as privileges and demanded a special sensitivity, perhaps also a certain catholicity, of response even where – indeed, perhaps especially where – the theorist's aggressive clarity and high-mindedness were likely to make themselves most keenly felt.

Secondly, he found in Zemlinsky a very particular combination of qualities which were those not just of a skilled and highly professional but of a profoundly self-aware and authentic musician – 'authentic' in the combined sense of being true both to himself and to the material he worked with. This entailed, in Adornian terms, a critical holding-in-balance of his own subjectivity and experience, on the one hand, with the collective dimension of the current 'state of musical art', on the other, keeping all the while a very clear consciousness of the potentialities and obligations of the available musical materials in their particular historical configuration at that time. That he appears to have responded to Zemlinsky as an authentic musician in this sense does not mean, however, that he would have considered him as being theoretically articulate in any very explicit way. If anything, the reverse was the case. In sharp contrast to Schoenberg, we generally lack strong theoretical pronouncements from Zemlinsky, and there is little to set beside the *Style and Idea* essays and other theorising texts from all periods of Schoenberg's life – even though we know that Schoenberg himself often pointedly sought Zemlinsky's advice in earlier years. Rather, we have to gather (and often infer) Zemlinsky's views from other sources, such as the correspondence of the Schoenberg circle or the reported evidence of colleagues and former pupils.[4]

And thirdly, for all the consequentiality and rigour of his observation and his arguments, Adorno undoubtedly had (as I suggested above) a somewhat freer sense of history and historical unfolding, especially so far as the cultural and social determinants of music and musical production and the scope for individual agency were concerned, than many readers have been inclined to suppose. This sense emerges only sporadically, it is true, at times even incidentally, and in any case seems rather surprising in an avowedly Marxist thinker. Yet it seems to have been a genuine if not very obvious facet of his understanding of the broader realities of history and collective culture in their relation to individual creative work and artistic production. And it was one that might well have been a product of his own personal dialectic – coming out of the conflicts and tensions of his own situation and experience, and reflecting something of the complexity of his position as an 'internal critic' of his times.

While a narrow Hegelian view of historical dialectic would have allowed a single line of cultural and artistic development to be seen as dominant (say, the Schoenbergian one), the broader and more flexible explanatory approach taken by thinkers contemporary with Adorno such as Walter Benjamin and Ernst Cassirer, took a looser and more open view of such things.[5] Their recognition of the complex origins and formation of cultural and artistic styles, and the extreme difficulty (not to say unrealism) of seeking to pin down such many-sided and in many ways mysterious phenomena to single, identifiable causes, gave them a freer, less theoretically driven perspective than is characteristic of Adorno.

If it was not just the chance of history and historical vicissitudes but also the force of a dominant historiography that, after 1945, served to narrow our vision of what was most viable in the musical art of the preceding decades, or most characteristic of it, then there is not merely a need but a necessity for us to reopen the question, first, of how such a view came into being, and second, of what a more realistic and balanced approach might consist in, and what new kinds of understanding it would make possible. In any event, it seems entirely justifiable to suggest *contra* Hegel that the 'timeliness' or otherwise of cultural and stylistic change is not built into the historical context as a given, but is, precisely, one of the variables that result from an open and inclusive model which is able to see a more all-encompassing breadth of historical development – that is to say, a plurality of developments coexisting and interacting, in a variety of ways, across any given period. And this is precisely the force of the phrase 'ways of the new' in the title of the present essay: that in the realm of cultural and artistic development there are always multiple determinants and possible outcomes; hence, that there are multiple individual responses to the 'state of musical art' and to the potentialities of the available musical materials; and that there must always be multiple paths (some of them no doubt Heideggerian *Holzwege*) leading to the production of the new. The idea of single-track historical necessity – a myth that the Schoenberg circle never really gave up – can in this way be replaced with a historiographical and interpretative model of broader sympathies and scope that allows space to consider the richness of the total picture, as well as the artistic self-assertion and achievement of gifted individuals.

But to return to the specific questions of the Zemlinsky case, we need to enquire what, aside from the fact of his talent and experience and the sheer *savoir-faire* he brought to his very varied musical activities, remains most strikingly and lastingly characteristic of his work when considered not in the shadow of Schoenberg, but in the light of history – whether that of Zemlinsky himself, or of our own.

Zemlinsky witnessed during his lifetime, as all his generation did, the breaking up and restructuring, across the length and breadth of Europe, of a social and cultural as well as a political and economic order. It is perhaps self evident that this process of often turbulent upheaval and change was stretched out over a considerable period of time and took on diversified forms in different places, thereby constituting the working out of a complex, long-range historical problem rather than a mere sequence of events, however dramatic and groundbreaking in themselves. Its relevance here is that we should see it not as a merely descriptive or picturesque background against which the drama of Zemlinsky's life and activity was played out, nor even as a set of conditioning factors (which it undoubtedly was), but more strongly still as part of the very stuff of that drama. The tensions that existed between the collective social – and institutional – forces of the musical culture of the time and the individual talents which sustained and drove it forward, were paralleled by those between the shared musical values of that culture, as such, and the social and economic factors by which its activities were governed and constrained. Such tensions were reflected, furthermore, in the struggles between conservative and progressive tendencies not only in society, politics and economics, but also in the arts, including the applied and performing arts.

It was the wide acceptance of a particular musical ethos that had made Austro-German music what it was, historically speaking, and given it the tremendous cultural energy and *élan* (and perhaps also the dominance) it enjoyed from the eighteenth through to the early years of the twentieth century.[6] In this sense it was the expression not just of individual visions or forms of artistry but of a shared tradition that had held together through all – and no doubt in part because of – its diversity. The richness of activity and invention was historically, and still remains in retrospect, a clear demonstration of the vitality of that tradition. Moreover it was a tradition that was founded – implicitly, because that was simply how things were, but also to an extent deliberately and self-consciously – on an ideal of complete, all-round musicianship. This was accepted as an intrinsic part of the way music was practised and transacted, and how it was integrated into general cultural and social life, in terms of educational provision, the mapping out of career paths, and the kinds of experiences that were felt to contribute in complementary ways to musical culture as a whole.

Conductors were often also composers and vice versa, at whatever musical level this might be, and all conductors were at the very least well versed in matters of instrumentation, of orchestral texture and sonority. Many of them were also active as pianists, especially accompanying singers or perhaps, on occasion, violinists: Artur Nikisch accompanied the young Elena Gerhardt as, later on, Bruno Walter accompanied Ferrier and Furtwängler accompanied Schwarzkopf, while George Szell began as a composer and was then a brilliant (and financially demanding) pianist, before becoming the famously exigent conductor he was to be for most of his career. Such examples could be multiplied many times over.[7] And into this multiple role, that of the charismatic music director, the energetic and adaptable Zemlinsky fitted very neatly. It was a tradition to which he was born, and in which he was raised. Hence it was to that extent a 'natural' condition for him, and he remained true to it in both a practical and an idealistic sense throughout his life.

Whatever kind of musical activity he was engaged in, Zemlinsky was known as someone who approached all the important things he did with a determined and very focused intentionality. Along with his characteristic drive and energy, as well as his sheer technical accomplishment, there was in him a fiercely committed – and in that sense radical – sense of musical purpose. And it was as present in his recreative and interpretative as in his original compositional work. The Prague critic Ernst Rychnovsky wrote of him in the summer of 1917, six years after he had first arrived in the city, with a clear understanding of this virtue: 'Those who know Zemlinsky's ways... know that he is an artist who does nothing that is not carefully considered'.[8] His observation was made primarily in regard to his conducting and his musical direction of the German Theatre in Prague (the Neues Deutsches Theater). But it seems clear that such was his attitude across the range of his artistic activities – so that this thorough, probing, energetic, brilliantly professional approach was equally evident in all his very varied musical tasks, whether he was coaching, rehearsing, accompanying (like Nikisch, Furtwängler and Walter, he was apparently a wonderful and enthusiastic Lieder accompanist), conducting, planning, programming or, finally, composing.

Far from being merely circumstantially determined, it was undoubtedly a characteristic of the man, one that arose in part out of his individual gifts and temperament, in part simply out of the kind of musician that he was. For surely one of the initial keys to unlocking the phenomenon (or rather let us say the mystery, for mystery there was, and is) of Zemlinsky is that we should see him not merely as an exemplary figure but as a singularly brilliant exponent of the Austro-German idea – and indeed not just the idea, but the living reality – of the all-round musician. As I have suggested, this rich and multifaceted tradition meant that a composer was typically first and foremost a working musician in the broadest sense, one who engaged in a spectrum of activities and was fully integrated into musical life, yet who happened to specialise in composition. Such was the case of Mahler. And in the most gifted musical personalities it is clear that this breadth brought with it not a weakening but rather a strengthening of compositional resourcefulness and invention, and certainly of cogency and fluency. That Zemlinsky in one way or another inherited this sense of musical vocation from his milieu, specifically from the transcendent example set by Mahler, seems overwhelmingly probable and is, I would argue, relatively easy to accept, historically and psychologically. But that it also represents in a more specific and personal way the preferences of Zemlinsky himself, as both man and musician, seems deeply relevant too. His preferred musical culture was a broad-based, intensely professional but also participatory one. And it was one, above all, in which the new was fully integrated with the old.

Adorno's Zemlinsky: a transformational and modernising eclecticism

Adorno hit upon a very neat and (it must be said) ingenious way of formulating his particular view of Zemlinsky's musical outlook and approach, one that gives us a useful tool for examining his work in relation to the wide range of late tonal or extended-tonal styles that coexisted the length and breadth of Germany and Austria during the years of the Weimar Republic. He heard Zemlinsky as inhabiting this shared late-tonal tradition not in a nostalgic or entrenched but rather in a distinctively modern, forward-looking way. He knew very well – partly by theory, but just as importantly from experience and observation, despite his generally anti-empiricist stance as a philosopher – that the progress of music in the years between 1890 and 1939 simply could not be limited to the schematic idea of a 'strong' linear descent from Wagner through Mahler to Schoenberg with 'weak' peripheral styles constellated vaguely around them, or else falling by the wayside entirely. The sheer variety of post-Wagnerian (and of course contra-Wagnerian) styles was self-evidently too great and too persistent for that. And in the case of Schoenberg, as in that of Zemlinsky, the problematisation of the constituent technical and stylistic elements (what we might call the 'Problemstellung' of the musical materials, their sources, and subsequent productivity) positively demanded that equal consideration and weight be given to Brahms and to Wagner.[9]

Adorno's *Philosophie der neuen Musik* (written 1941–8, published Tübingen, 1949) had famously set up Schoenberg and Stravinsky – before the death of the former, and thus before the latter's adoption of serial technique – as the polarised extremes of the New Music. Several of the shorter critical essays (such as those on Schreker and Zemlinsky, which, having been devised as broadcast talks in 1959, were first published in 1963 in the collection *Quasi una fantasia*) seem to have fulfilled the purpose of then fleshing out in greater detail the broad evolutionary process of which the two great figures were seen as the main agents. Also implicated in this fleshing out were the monographs on Wagner (1952), Mahler (1960) and Berg (1968), which extended and diversified the historical scope of the model he had begun to construct.

Viewed in this way, one might see the work of the last ten years or so of Adorno's thinking and writing career as representing a sustained effort to see in a clearer and more realistic light the complexity and diversity of the historical-dialectical picture he had set out to elaborate. The more difficult question of the kinds of modifications this may have brought to his theorising can probably best be addressed by considering the extraordinary, at times almost labyrinthine achievement of the unfinished *Ästhetische Theorie* (written and worked on over the course of a decade, and posthumously published in 1970).[10] Essays such as the studies of Schreker and Zemlinsky, then, may be seen in the first place as Adorno's way of working out some of the possible implications of a more flexible and broad-based understanding of the evolutionary course of musical modernity, drawing as he did so on a variety of materials and observation – the result of all this being, in the end, a more balanced view of the very varied 'ways of the new' that did not prioritise any one strand as uniquely dominant, but saw it instead in a broader perspective, as part of a larger cultural picture.

Adorno's starting point was that, although Zemlinsky's work did indeed exhibit the fundamentally eclectic approach to extended-tonal composition that was common to a relatively large group of composers of the pre-Second World War period, his use of it was of a very particular kind. By the degree of creative intensity aroused in him in response to his models and source styles, he was able to interiorise and transform these given materials in a potentially radical way that was of a wholly different order from mere borrowing, appropriation or citation:

> But [Zemlinsky's] eclecticism becomes the stuff of genius through the
> intensification of [his gift of] receptivity to the point of a truly seismographic
> reactive power in the face of all the [musical] stimuli by which he lets himself be
> inundated.[11]

This gift, as described by Adorno, appears to be a psychological quality quite
as much as – and perhaps more than – a musical technique or set of techniques.
His response to the given and available materials was qualitatively different
from that of other, less intensely receptive, musicians. And it was precisely the
'seismographic' shock waves produced in him through the psychological process of
reception (*Reaktionsfähigkeit*) that conditioned – and in Adorno's view enhanced
– his subsequent creative production. Adorno thus allowed for Zemlinsky's use
of traditional materials, but ascribed to him a quality of mind and temperament
which marked out his personal version of the eclectic as something rather special,
indeed quite out of the ordinary, and which was moreover audibly present in his
music. These audible traces were perceptible, Adorno suggested, as newly inventive
musical formulations which he described as 'impulses' (*Impulse*) but which we might
also characterise (a little fancifully, perhaps) as 'sparks of the modern'. It was these
features, then, which constituted an important part of Zemlinsky's contribution to
the evolutionary process of modern music, despite the fact that his particular form
of musical modernity was quickly overtaken and eclipsed by new and much more
radical developments. The immediate result of this was that its cultural energy and
its capacity to radiate influence in any appreciable way quickly waned. And yet it was
precisely through these 'sparks' or 'impulses' that his music retained its actuality and
its power of communication:

> [T]he force-field of his musical output has preserved its actuality for precisely
> the reason that the great so-called 'developmental' or 'progressive tendency' [of the
> first half of the twentieth century] overtook it and passed it by completely. Like
> few other kinds of music, Zemlinsky's contains within itself impulses which
> brought the new into [vital] movement, but which were then superseded and got
> left behind – although their very sacrifice expresses something of the price that had
> to be paid for the cogent progress (*für den konsequenten Fortschritt*) [i.e. of music
> as a whole]. This [price] was that of the clear formation of vivid individual musical
> characters.[12]

It was his special talent for finding and articulating these 'individual characters'
in his compositions that was one of the many things that enabled (and still
enable) Zemlinsky to stand *out* – and just as importantly, I would suggest, stand
apart – from the Schoenbergian triumvirate. He had quite consciously preserved
these *Einzelcharaktere* as an important communicative element of his musical

language, whereas the expressionist-modernists had to a great extent abandoned them in favour of a musical continuity of sustained hyper-expressivity in which everything was overlaid with complex, dissonant layers of elaboration, of an intensificatory kind.[13] Furthermore, Zemlinsky in no way lagged behind Schoenberg in the acuteness of his response to the available musical materials of the era. Rather the contrary – for it was he, Adorno suggested, who had first discerned and then set out the limits and broad contours of the field in which those materials could be seen to coexist and interact:

> If in the work of Schoenberg the most divergent impulses of the period commingled and, in flowing together, [ultimately] gave rise to the idea of constructive composition, then it was Zemlinsky who defined the limits and topography of the musical culture in which those impulses could relate to one another on an equal basis – apart from Wagner and Brahms there were above all Mahler, and Debussy, and Schoenberg. But this should not be taken to refer to the mere external fact of an informed composer's awareness of the most significant so-called 'tendencies of the time'. Rather, Zemlinsky's right to be heard *as that which made him what he always was to his Viennese friends* is grounded in the fact that, in his [compositional] work, those very forces already [interact and] work themselves out in a very productive way.[14]

And here – rather surprisingly, in an almost understated way – we find ourselves close to the heart of Adorno's understanding of the Zemlinsky phenomenon. He saw him as a musician who, having drawn on the 'most divergent impulses of the period'[15] and made good use of them (since they had been made to 'work themselves out in a very productive way'), had thereby earned himself the right to be listened to for that which he was, and which his fellow musicians in Vienna knew and believed him to be – an original and forward-looking composer, working in a strong and inventive way with the given musical materials of the period, within a broadly modernising but not a radical-atonal perspective. This was what characterised him as modern in his own time; and it still has the power to characterise him as modern to present-day listeners. For Zemlinsky was just as concerned, in his own way, about the 'advancement of the language' as the Second Viennese composers were – Berg and Webern in particular seem to have recognised this fact, even though he (Zemlinsky) operated as a composer in a perceptibly different way from them, and especially, perhaps, from Schoenberg.

But can we get any closer to what this modernity and originality might have consisted in? Adorno saw the growth of new and viable musical formulations, in a gestural and structural as well as in a more conventionally thematic and stylistic sense, as emerging not from the cautious negotiation of a weak compromise between two extremes (in the interests of a false and attenuated ideal of harmonious synthesis), but rather from the intensive working out of the tendencies and implications of those very extremes through a strong, autonomous process:

> Not for nothing does the word 'synthesis', as the opposing idea to both mannerism and eclecticism, sound flat and weak. For the mediation of divergent [ideas and materials] comes about only through the extremes, not through a conciliating balance [between them].[16]

This ideal – simultaneously formal *and* expressive – of the mediation of divergent forces and ideas, and their working out through the whole range of their interaction (including the extremes, therefore), found its greatest embodiment in the work of Beethoven. And despite subsequent Romantic preoccupations with poetic content and evocation, with the poetic characterisation of themes and paragraphs, and with narrative, this idea of the supreme value of an intrinsically musical unfolding structure remained a desideratum and indeed a possible goal right the way through until 1939. Thus, in propitious circumstances, the Beethovenian ideal could remain viable and alive, even in the midst of the great modernist/conservative struggles of the interwar years. One particularly interesting and effective way in which Zemlinsky and others were able, even in an extended- or non-tonal context, to extend the scope of this ideal was in the structuring of a movement of sonata type around a contrast not just of themes and thematic manipulations but of two alternating tempi, with all the interesting tensions and fluctuations that could be set up between them – as happens for example in the first movement of the Third Quartet.[17].

The attainment of a sense of finality within a musical work was in this sense not just a dialectical journey through conflicting extremes to reach a formal conclusion[18] but also, just as importantly, something more akin to a cathartic process: often tough, always taut and focused, even when in lyric mode, and with a sense of arrival and release at the end. The kind of musical process – technical, structural, expressive – that Adorno envisaged was not so much smoothly integrated as intensive and intensificatory, implicitly dramatic (or at least powerfully argumentative) even when the character of the material might seem to call for a looser, more expansive treatment. Zemlinsky's music in his maturity fulfils this aim, partly through his extraordinarily strong and detailed motivic-thematic working, partly through his espousal of the principle of developing variation – including a very individual mastery of roving harmony that is nevertheless tonally framed. A number of clear and straightforward examples of this can be found, understandably, in the earlier works. But the phenomenon becomes even more striking in the later music where the boundaries of tonal cohesion, of good thematic continuation and the conventional distribution of material, are often considerably stretched. As Beaumont observes, the Fourth Quartet of 1936 deploy[s] an untypically large number of themes and motifs in uncharacteristically open-ended structures. As in the [Berg] *Lyric Suite*, the proportions of the movements are irregular [and] several sections stretch the concept of tonal harmony beyond breaking point.[19]

And yet the working out of the materials, the implied cadential drift or undertow, and the concluding gestures of each of the six movements taken together represent, in every case, an audible and distinctive tonal catharsis of some kind, albeit one of varying degrees of finality. This practical and largely intuitive approach to the question of extended tonality on Zemlinsky's part was keenly appreciated, and briefly described for posterity by his brilliant pupil, Erich Wolfgang Korngold.[20].

Perhaps the point at which Adorno's essay displays the keenest (and for us most revealing) appreciation of Zemlinsky's contribution is in his discussion of two works, separated by nearly a decade, which lie at the heart of his narrative: the String Quartet No. 3, Op. 19 (1924) and the orchestral *Sinfonietta*, Op. 23 (1934). These were arguably the years – also the most fruitful and productive years of the ISCM, and his own involvement with it – in which the modernity of Zemlinsky's music was most clearly marked out for contemporary listeners. The composition of the Third Quartet seems to have arisen directly out of his experience of the death of his sister, Mathilde, in 1923, followed by Schoenberg's swift remarriage to Gertrud Kolisch the following year;[21] while the *Sinfonietta* was the immediate product of a period of new-found – and of course very unaccustomed – leisure in the spring of 1934, after his return to Vienna from Berlin the previous autumn.[22]

The Third Quartet is radical, unarguably one of Zemlinsky's most radical works, and for the most part strikingly concise. It also enters what was for him a wholly new sound-world. Beaumont aptly remarks that it 'represents a complete break' with the kind of music most readily associated with his 'natural artistic habitat' – music that might be summarily described as latently Brahmsian, or perhaps Fuchsian (in workmanship); aesthetically Secessionist (in form and figure); and emotionally Tristanesque (in its sustained expressive intensity). But the Third Quartet was different: it drove these characteristics underground, distilled them away into (at times) almost nothing, into the merest quintessence of what his rich and fiery quartet writing had been in the Second Quartet Op. 15 of 1913–15. Not that the principles of construction and expression had been entirely swept away, simply that they had been made to work systematically beyond the reach of their usual limits of operation.

Sonically, then, the new quartet emerged from almost nowhere; and its expressive world, too, was nearly as unforeseen – if the work was indeed a response to Mathilde's death (as circumstances overwhelmingly indicate that it was), then its tragic/elegiac burden was almost miraculously transformed into a voyage of discovery – for in this piece Zemlinsky may be said to have rediscovered anew, for himself, the myriad possibilities of quartet texture. Not only that, but he discovered almost for the first time (even the artful subtleties and simplicities of the *Maeterlinck Songs* cannot match it in this respect) a new kind of musical continuity built as much on allusiveness of texture and contour and melodic gesture, often on the very smallest scale, as on any more conventional type of linear or thematic evolution. The special effects of string sonority, in the individual parts as in the quartet texture as a whole, are extraordinary, and must surely owe more, as Beaumont astutely suggests, to Zemlinsky's exposure to new ideas at the early ISCM chamber music festivals than to any other source.[23] The range of textural colours and combinations stands somewhere between those of the two-movement Berg Op. 3 quartet (composed 1910), on the one hand, and those of the short Webern pieces contained in Op. 5 (composed 1909) and the even shorter ones in Op. 9 (composed 1911–13), on the other.[24] But the tone is, as ever, utterly individual, and quite distinct from any of these. Somewhat less vehement and intense than the Berg, though with perhaps a greater range of expression, it has a palette that moves between the extremes of contemplation and passion, and certainly has more pointed humour than the Berg. Zemlinsky's textures are new and experimental, but not as extreme as those in the Webern Op. 5 pieces and, especially, the Op. 9 Bagatelles. Overall, the mystery and ambiguity of the quartet's expressive burden, along with its extreme technical and stylistic subtlety, make it surely one of the great chamber music works of the interwar years.

The *Sinfonietta*, an exhilarating three-movement work of blinding originality and freshness, has nevertheless a stylistic and aesthetic positioning that is profoundly historical, for all that Zemlinsky may rightly be said to have arrived at this creative moment along his own very individual path.[25] It is a work which is in the deepest sense rooted and located, though it also strikes us, in perception, as autonomous and free. It is moreover a work of striking expressive conviction – mercurial, at times humorous and witty, always purposeful and energetic (even at a slow tempo, as in the central 'Ballade' in B flat minor), yet at the same time deeply considered. To put it another way, we might say that it speaks freely and directly as living musical utterance, wholly in the present, yet in full knowledge of its own past:

> Overall, the *Sinfonietta* takes its place within that area of [musical] production in which a by now confident and self-aware modernism begins to play [once more] with the long-buried schemata and formal archetypes of Viennese classicism, enabling them to shine forth in all freedom and independence, while at the same time using them for its own catharsis.[26]

This is a cultural moment which finds its true exponent, its true champion perhaps, in Zemlinsky. Here is not only an individual artistic creation of joyous brilliance and fluency as well as structural tautness (the three movements together last around 20 minutes), but a work which plays without any special sense of irony – and certainly not of alienation – on the recognition of its own historical position. It takes on tradition directly, without having to frame or caricature it first. It does not disown the chromatic and expressionistic journey that had led up to it, but takes this experience forward into a freer musical world that is less obviously bound to exigencies of intensive psychological (and indeed psychodramatic) representation. Above all, its harmonic and thematic idiom is effortlessly original, audibly so, without any hint of working from a derived or satirised style. Perhaps only a musician such as Zemlinsky, with equal gifts in conducting and composition, and a profoundly empirical knowledge of how orchestral music can be made to sound and unfold to maximum effect with a minimum of calculation, could have achieved this with such apparent ease. (Hindemith at his best, and perhaps the earlier Weill, too, are others who spring to mind, and for similar reasons.)

We should not expect Zemlinsky to have theorised this in words and concepts, however. He was a musician who composed freely, often no doubt intuitively, in whatever situation he found himself, within the limits of his own vision and technique and of his innate capacity to feel all these musical relationships at their full value. But unlike Schoenberg (or Adorno, or maybe even Stravinsky), he lacked a strong theorising impulse, and wrote remarkably little about such things, even in letters – he was deeply self-reflexive as both man and artist (by nature, by habit, and I suspect also by inclination), but not in an overtly theoretical way. Others, notably Korngold as we have seen, reported on the illuminating remarks he would make in composition lessons, while demonstrating some point of 'local theory' that was relevant to the problem at hand. And these remarks, fleeting though they usually are, have for us a range and a reach, and above all a suggestive power that may serve to open up vistas far beyond the narrow confines of what is usually thought of as music theory. Yet the overriding impression is of a musician who knew himself, and clearly valued the insights that came to him from whatever source, but who took his decisions and worked on his projects largely without *a priori* theorising.

For Adorno, then, the *Sinfonietta* is knowing and self aware (*wissend*), but not parodically so. It does not caricature its sources, nor does it seek to pin down or 'capture' its models. Instead it uses – or rather, inhabits – their world actively and dynamically. It plays in a free and energetic way with the elements of an older classicism in a very special way that might be described, if the phrase will serve, as still classical rather than newly classical. An apt comparison here might be with the Beethoven of the Eighth Symphony Op. 93 of 1812 and the Op. 135 quartet of 1826. For these two Beethovenian works – not unlike the *Sinfonietta* in this respect – find a way of re-engaging with the manner of late Haydn, or with that of Beethoven's own first maturity as it had emerged around 1800, without renouncing the wonderful thematic, textural and rhythmic acquisitions of the intervening years. Both composers wear their musical (and human) knowledge lightly, moving without apparent effort from the witty and humorous to a realm of pathos and intensity rapidly, with no sense of incongruity – in this sense it would be plausible to suggest that the *Sinfonietta* stands, in spirit, as close to the First as to the Second Viennese School.

In this way, Adorno concludes, the *Sinfonietta* may be said to stand as a key example of a subtly new conception of form (*Formgesinnung*) that Zemlinsky had arrived at along an individual and no doubt largely intuitive path. This new conception of musical form and figure, and of the kinds of thematic elements and processes that could go to make it up, marked it out quite clearly from the more intellectually self-conscious position of the neoclassicists:

> At the same time, Zemlinsky's *Sinfonietta* has nothing in common with the neoclassicism of the followers of Stravinsky. It neither assumes an archaic stasis, nor parodies that which already belongs to the past. Rather, it juggles so buoyantly, and with such extreme facility, with the [elements of the] inherited form that the insistent demands [of this form] never come into collision with the melodically differentiated flow of events. [Thus] Zemlinsky's taste results finally in a sense of form that prefers to master the prohibitive difficulties of symphonism for the present day by means of omission and deft avoidance – [an approach] which does not look back, fiercely and earnestly, towards the past, but equally, avoids the risk of attempting new [methods of] through-composition in a symphonic spirit.[27]

This vision of the *Sinfonietta* seems to point up the parallel, suggested above, with the Beethovenian turn to overtly classicising forms which yet remained in full possession of the radicalised (and radicalising) knowledge of what had gone before – in Beethoven's case, those musical revelations which came from the late period beginning, say, with the Piano Sonata in A, Op. 101 and the Cello Sonatas, Op. 102, not forgetting a quick look backwards at the F minor String Quartet, Op. 95 and *An die ferne Geliebte*, Op. 98; in Zemlinsky's case from the time of the Third Quartet and the *Symphonische Gesänge*, Op. 20, with a retrospective glance back towards the *Maeterlinck Songs*, Op. 13 (1910–13) of more than a decade earlier.[28]

Zemlinsky and his contemporaries: composing, conducting, and the idea of an integrated musical culture

And so, finally, we shall invoke once more the opinions and the words of others, from across a slightly broader spectrum. Speaking from close to the end of his life, Stravinsky clearly still revered – and without doubt owed much to, for these were revelatory experiences – the theatre performances he was able to hear Zemlinsky conduct in Prague, notably of *Der Freischütz* and *Le Nozze di Figaro*.[29]

[M]y appreciation of Weber did not come until the 1920s, with a performance of *Der Freischütz* in Prague conducted by Alexander von Zemlinsky... [And I also] remember a *Marriage of Figaro* led by him in Prague as one of the most satisfying operatic experiences of my life.

There is no mention here, not even so much as a hint, of Zemlinsky's activity as a composer: he is classed, unambiguously, with the executants.[30] He is seen – very positively, it must be said – as a committed and profoundly musical conductor whose interpretative work was exemplary, at times revelatory, and hence as essential to musical life in its totality as was the contribution of any composer. But there is no acknowledgement at all of his creative output. It is clear that this is how many musicians of the interwar years, and probably most of the public too (certainly the public at large), must have regarded him. And if we may with justification regret, once again, the apparent lack of recognition for the composer, while taking pleasure in the high praise given to the achievement of his conducting, the story it serves to reinforce is the familiar one of a musical culture which was of a far higher degree of integration and artistic selflessness than has been usual since 1945 – however strenuous the efforts may have been to recreate such a culture in renewed guise during the later 1940s and 50s and afterwards.

Here, then, we may momentarily pause to consider the historical position and reputation of such iconic figures, more or less contemporary with Zemlinsky, as Klemperer, Furtwängler, Bruno Walter, and other musicians of similar type. If it was, in retrospect, their historical destiny to have transmitted a certain tradition of conducting the Austro-German repertory to the post-war world, through a combination of concerts and recordings (and in many cases too through their exodus from central Europe), then this achievement came, in the end, at the expense of their own compositional work. Their legacy was in the form not of the contribution of further repertory pieces, of whatever degree of mastery, to add to the already great operatic and orchestral archive, but rather in the form of a timeless demonstration of the fundamentally (re)creative power of the conductor's interpretative work, rightly understood and entered into – of interpretation, that is, which is fully adequate in depth and detail to the music it addresses.[31] And this happened despite the fact that writing music was still, for most of them, an integral part of their professional vocation, of a complete musical life as they understood it, and of all that it meant to be a musician in the largest sense.

Yet despite the similarities, Zemlinsky was not made in quite the same mould. For all that he rubbed shoulders with his colleagues, musically speaking, and worked alongside them in much the same kinds of roles and functions, his commitment to – or better perhaps: his drive towards – composing was stronger, maybe also more fanatical and (in the best sense) obsessive than theirs; and his output was more evenly weighted between the opera house, the chamber music room and the concert

hall than, for example, was Mahler's. Furthermore, he lacked the egocentric impulse
that motivated many – though of course not all – of the more successful career
'Dirigenten' (as opposed to the 'mere' Kapellmeister) of the interwar years. This lack
of a strong egocentric impulse (his lack of useful elbows, as he once memorably put
it to Alma Mahler)[32] may perhaps have been something of an inhibiting factor in
his creative and compositional activity, or at least in his not very effective approach
to self-promotion; but it was surely what was responsible, at least in part, for his
extraordinary recreative and interpretative gifts, especially in contemporary music,
where he was clearly able to identify to a quite remarkable degree with new and
unfamiliar work, and put himself and his capacities entirely at the service of the
'other' composer. There can be little doubt that he regarded this as an integral part
of his artistic vocation.

The combined result of all this was that the sphere of conducting and direction,
even though it took up so much of his time and energy and in return gave him
the economic means of survival, nevertheless could not extinguish the flame of
his compositional fire except through illness, the frisson of seeing mortality, and,
finally, death itself. Composition was a source of self-renewal, both creative *and*
psychological, and fulfilled other needs too. At moments of crisis, for example, he
seems to have retreated into music, or to have searched through it for some kind of
an experience – perhaps largely indirect, and certainly without the aid of words or
received ideas – of spiritual depth and catharsis. (The case of the death of his sister
and the Third Quartet offers the prime example here, along with that of the Fourth
Quartet as a wordless, but deeply eloquent, memorial to Berg.)[33] In all this as in so
much else the tacit example remained, throughout his life, that of Mahler. And if,
like Mahler, he sought with all the human resilience and energy at his command
to encompass as full a range of musical activities as possible, then the primary
importance of the compositional output, as both vision and legacy, was absolute and
never in doubt, whatever the vicissitudes of worldly recognition and success.

Schoenberg's published tribute to Zemlinsky, dating from 1921 (hence before
the great rift that came between the two men following the death of Mathilde
in 1923), makes the centrality of this compositional vocation quite clear.[34] For
unlike Stravinsky he writes of Zemlinsky, with all that strange and rather awkward
atmosphere of reticence and ambiguity that this text seems to hint at, and which
it is not difficult for us to sense behind his words, pre-eminently as a composer
– more particularly as one who, for all his 'masterly talent', had scarcely yet come
into his own. And he writes almost exclusively in terms of the opera theatre and the
operatic composer, as if to indicate beyond doubt what ought to have been the site
of Zemlinsky's most important public achievements as it was, for example, that of
Schreker's at that very period.[35]

More generally, Schoenberg praised Zemlinsky's many 'virtues which have grown
since I first began to appreciate them', and emphasised what he called 'my good and

lasting idea of him' – an idea which may or may not have outlasted the break in their friendship, but which is not so often encountered later on in any such explicit form. It is clearly true that they never forgot or lost respect for one another – how could they have done? – and we find a number of later instances where brief reference is made to the inextricable, and in musical terms obviously ineradicable, closeness of their rapport. One striking example of this, not from either of them but from a knowledgeable 'third party Schoenbergian', is to be found in the quick, humorous aside elicited from Dika Newlin by her transient encounter with a broadcast performance of the *Sinfonietta* given by the New York Philharmonic in late 1940 (while Zemlinsky was still alive, therefore):

> 29 December 1940: [...] [the *Sinfonietta*] seems a very fine work: solid, spirited, and often quite Schoenbergian. One sees where S. learned some of his cute tricks, all right![36]

The playfulness evident in this remark is disarming, as well as revealing; for it is difficult – most would say impossible – to imagine Schoenberg himself ever conceding anything similar in so candid a way, still less tolerating the idea that he ever used 'cute tricks'. What Schoenberg's balanced evaluation of his true debt to Zemlinsky – or even of the *Sinfonietta* itself, as a composition of manifest brilliance and originality that was audibly modern as well as 'in tradition' – might have been, we can only guess. Perhaps Schoenberg's own psychological conflicts would scarcely even have allowed him to envisage straightforward answers to such questions.

Leaving aside the enigmatic (and inevitably much quoted) phrase 'Zemlinsky can wait',[37] the most intriguing and perhaps most suggestive passage in Schoenberg's tribute is where he addresses the question of listening and response – what one might call the 'possible truths' of musical experience. He muses on the possibility for a composer (implicitly Zemlinsky) of attaining 'that [kind of musical] language in which one can express oneself so that everyone thinks they understand' but which also contains much that is subtle and inwardly complex – an approach, that is, in which the composer manages '[t]o say everything, and yet to keep it so secret that the theatre-goer never meets with anything that might disturb him'.[38] Perhaps, here, there is a hint of longing on Schoenberg's part for a comprehensiblity that he would himself have wished for, but which he found instead in far greater measure in Zemlinsky – though of course without its having brought him (Zemlinsky) any of the recognition and success he should by rights have enjoyed. For there is little doubt that Schoenberg wished passionately all his life for an acceptance and a recognition grounded in such comprehensibility. Almost in spite of this, however, and in deep conflict with it, the profound musical explorations which led him through the adventure of atonality to serialism effectively put him beyond the reach of any broad-based or popular appreciation.[39] Consequently, his recognition of such a potential, even though unrealised, in Zemlinsky's music would all too easily have aroused in him (understandably suppressed) symptoms of something uncomfortably close to sibling rivalry. And the fact that Zemlinsky had himself explicitly refused the atonal adventure could not but have sharpened this.

Yet Schoenberg's observation is an acute and illuminating one, whatever its particular slant or its undeclared subtext; and we are surely justified in extending it from the realm of the operatic to that of the instrumental and orchestral music, to which it relates with equal if not greater force. For it is true that Zemlinsky's musical surfaces are so beautifully crafted, so fluently articulated and energised at every level from the detail of the motif or the phrase to the periodicity of the larger form, that it is all too easy to miss, for example, the quite extraordinarily skilled pacing and the tautness of the constituent detail (of a rhythmic and textural as well as a thematic and harmonic kind) which serve to control the flow of events. Examples of such an approach abound in the longer dramatic paragraphs of the operas and can be seen, too, in the instrumental and orchestral music. They are especially clear in the composer's supremely well-judged use of momentum and contour as a primary expression of a movement's shape or trajectory, serving to influence and modify, often quite radically, the expected thematic or harmonic articulations of the form.

Such an approach was not by any means unique to Zemlinsky;[40] but he used it in sophisticated and often undemonstrative ways that do not necessarily advertise themselves. A characteristic example may be found in the subtle and elusive 'Thema und Variationen' of the Third Quartet, where the irregular periodicity and fluctuating textures of the various phrases and sections within the variation scheme seem to arise in the first place chiefly from expressive (and perhaps psychological) considerations, rather than from any formal or structural features of the theme itself. In any case, there is very little of a theme as such to speak of in this movement. It could even be argued that the 'theme' is more adumbrated and implied by its own variations than elaborated by them – so that we might describe them as being in search of their (unstated) thematic origins and harmonic background rather than seeing them, in a more conventional way, as varied extensions or projections of an initial statement. (A possible, though stylistically very different parallel to this extraordinary movement can be found in the expressively clear, yet formally elusive, slow movement in D flat major, 'Lento assai, cantante e tranquillo', of Beethoven's String Quartet in F, Op. 135.) What does seem clear, however, is that Zemlinsky has a very purposeful sense, whatever genre he is working in, of forming his movements out of a well-judged – and always dynamic – equilibrium established between the evolutionary logic of the musical materials, on the one hand, and a freely unfolding expressive contour, on the other. These may run counter to one another, or in parallel; most of the time they coexist in a (very productive) state of fluctuating tension – such flexibility being precisely part of their attraction and their musical force. It is this kind of technical process that creates the intensity curves by which his music lives.

The play of sonority – in the simplest Lied accompaniment as in the most elaborate orchestral texture – is so keenly and vividly imagined and is kept, most of the time, within such well-judged limits, that it can blind us to the intrinsic force of the underlying invention. Yet the tautness and clarity of especially the later instrumental and orchestral textures, for all the brilliance and the eloquent sense of colour (primary, as well as mixed) so tellingly displayed, for example, in the *Symphonische Gesänge*, Op. 20 or the *Sinfonietta*, do not remain the only aural focus. Their function is to articulate the thought and to draw the ear into experiencing the musical substance, with which they are entirely fused.[41] Zemlinsky's mode of musical thought is one in which sound and gesture and idea are fully identified and always demand equal aural attention, even though it is the manipulation of timbre and the control of the orchestra, handled with an almost effortless skill, that most insistently strike and beguile the ear.

It is in this sense, then, that Zemlinsky's musical surfaces might be said to court the risk of deceiving the ear as much as they flatter it. For although his instrumentation is as exciting and resourceful as that of any composer in that brilliantly gifted generation, it is all too easy, as with Schreker but if anything more so, to take the timbral combinations and effects of sonority as bearers of meaning in their own right, without feeling the need to search beyond them for anything else. Zemlinsky's sound, like Schreker's or Berg's (or Dukas's, for that matter), is of course a primary dimension of his compositions, wonderfully beautiful (like theirs), and deeply characteristic of him. But what makes the music great and above all distinctive lies elsewhere, too, not only in sonority. It is the fusion of horizons (*Horizontverschmelzung*, to use Gadamer's term) between sound and idea, between the timbral or textural effects and the linear and thematic design, that makes this music, characteristically, what it is.

And it is surely something akin to this idea – one close to it, perhaps, or an extension of it – that lay behind Schoenberg's surprising, and otherwise inexplicable, remark about the difficulty of fully comprehending the Zemlinsky phenomenon in its fullest, furthest sense. In setting out (he is discussing the stage works) to 'consider why it is so hard to assess him adequately', he freely admits that 'the power of his music can open up vistas [far] wider than those of the stage'.[42] Yet he explicitly warns his readers, and by implication the listeners of the future too, not to relax too much and especially not to dare to listen inattentively, but to ensure they remember

> how hard to understand it all is, when one has only good ears and mind... [and] why even I, who am in good practice, must listen repeatedly in order to perceive this beauty and fullness.[43]

What on earth could this mean? Is Schoenberg admitting to not properly understanding Zemlinsky? Or perhaps to a wilful incapacity to fathom his own 'expert' perceptions? Berg and Webern both adored and admired the 'genuine Zemlinsky tone', and neither of them sought to polemicise or restrict or qualify his response in a negative way. Schoenberg's praise of other composers is by contrast so often backhanded, convoluted or hedged round with qualifications that it is all too easy for us not to perceive the true nature and purpose of his observation. In this case, he is not asserting that Zemlinsky is 'difficult' in the negative sense of being obscure or wilful or tortuous, but rather that his ease and fluency of manner, and his seemingly effortless command of *métier* (as observed on by Adorno), in some way belie the depth and intellectuality – most importantly, perhaps, the latent richness of meaning and the evolutionary modernity – of the music taken as a whole.

Surely, this remark of Schoenberg's is one of the more profound compliments paid by one composer to another – not one, to be sure, on a par with Haydn's famous tribute to Mozart or with Schumann's to Brahms, but a genuine and far-reaching one nevertheless. Schoenberg is saying something to the effect that the unforced energy of rhythm and invention and the keenly imagined sonic beauty of Zemlinsky's finest music endow it with a captivating immediacy, and a vividly suggestive power, but that the composer's technical capacity, and above all his expressive vision, are by no means exhausted in his concern for sonority and rhythmic movement. His sheer fluency of invention and the sounds he creates in such profusion are wonderful, but they are not by any means the music's whole story. As listeners we take keen pleasure in the kind of immediate listening experience it offers us, and are willingly carried along by this means; but its depths are not fully sounded out by such a mode of reception. Rather, they remain richly, implicitly present in – yet at the same time somehow also beyond – the very sonorities in which they are expressed and thus made present to us. Ultimately, perhaps, they remain a kind of mystery: 'how hard to understand it all is … this beauty and fullness' (in Schoenberg's words).

In the world of sound and close listening, then, as also in that mysterious, still largely uncharted realm of experience in which listening and feeling are as one, Zemlinsky's music has much to reveal, and perhaps to teach as well. Above all, in the hands of a true interpreter, far beyond the reach of any misplaced nostalgia or sentimentality, it has the power to strengthen and enchant.

Nur wer die Leier schon hob	Only he who once has raised
auch unter Schatten,	his lyre among the dead,
darf das unendliche Lob	can utter visionary praise,
ahnend erstatten.	foreknowing, without end.
Nur wer mit Toten vom Mohn	Only he who has eaten of
aß, von dem ihren,	the poppies of the dead
wird nicht den leisesten Ton	will never lose those quiet tones
wieder verlieren.	of subtlest intent.[44]

Notes

1   The two essays are published in Adorno, Theodor W (1997) *Gesammelte Schriften*, ed.
Rolf Tiedemann, 20 vols (Frankfurt am Main: Suhrkamp-Taschenbuch Wissenschaft),
vol. 16, pp.351–67 and 368–81. They first appeared in print in *Quasi una fantasia* (1963),
but originated as radio talks for the Norddeutscher Rundfunk (December 1959) and
Hessischer Rundfunk (March 1959) respectively.

2   See Wattenberger, R (2002) 'A "Very German Process": The Contexts of Adorno's Strauss
Critique', *19th-Century Music* xxv/2–3, pp.313–36. Evidence of their mistrust of the
Straussian aesthetic occurs from time to time in the correspondence of the Schoenberg
circle despite their general admiration for his professionalism and skill. Berg in particular
confided to Adorno something of his own reservations: see Adorno, Theodor W (1984)
Aesthetic Theory, ed. Gretel Adorno and Rolf Tiedemann (orig. Ger. edn 1972), Eng.
trans. Christian Lenhardt. London and New York: Routledge and Kegan Paul, p.306:
'One might, for instance, argue that Richard Strauss was a good technician, if nothing
else. Asked if he thought this was the case, Alban Berg once pointed out to me the
arbitrariness of Strauss's technique, [which] consists in putting together a number
of calculated effects which are however entirely unrelated in purely musical terms...
[Yet] Berg's technical critique of [what are] highly technical compositions seems to
disregard the view that Strauss [seems to have] intended to hypostatise the principle... It
is therefore plausible to argue that Berg's objection was [in fact] extraneous, that it was
informed by the perspective of the Schönberg school with its postulate of developmental
variation (which in turn was an anachronistic piece of traditionalism marshalled against
tradition [itself]). But this defence makes little aesthetic sense, [and in my view] Berg's
critique of Strauss's *métier* still holds'.

3   The committed, in general also very sympathetic involvement of both Berg and Webern
with the reception, and to an extent with the advocacy and promotion, of Zemlinsky's
music is clear at many junctures. It extended from coaching and the supervision of
quartet rehearsals to accompanying Lieder and ensuring that the Third Quartet would
be performed at the ISCM festival in 1928: see *inter alia* Beaumont, Antony (2000)
Zemlinsky. London: Faber and Faber, pp.274 and 330–2.

4   Korngold's valuable recollections were reported in the special Zemlinsky number of *Der
Auftakt* issued in October 1921 (compare Beaumont, 2000, pp.149–50 and n. 23). This
publication, for the composer's fiftieth birthday, also contained the Schoenberg tribute
'Gedanken über Zemlinsky', later republished in English, under the title 'Zemlinsky',
in Schoenberg, Arnold (1975) *Style and Idea*, ed. Leonard Stein and trans. Leo Black.
London: Faber and Faber, pp.486–7.

5   Ernst Cassirer (1874–1945) and Walter Benjamin (1892–1940). Cassirer's great
achievement was to have arrived at a philosophy of culture that combined a view of art
as symbolic form, in a profound sense (*Philosophy of Symbolic Forms*, 3 vols, 1923–1929,
highly influential on Susanne Langer), with an essentially phenomenological approach

to knowledge and expression/perception. Hence his view of culture would in principle
have allowed a variety of contributions as equally valid, to the extent that they each made
viable contributions to the living 'expressive function' of artistic forms. For the idea of
'*Problemgeschichte*' as a historical tradition of enquiry in which the course of history
can be viewed, and investigated, as the working out of a range of medium- and long-term
problems, see Oexle, Otto Gerhard (ed.) (2001) *Das Problem der Problemgeschichte 1880–
1932*. Göttingen: Wallstein Verlag.

6   For the earlier history of this tradition as a background to later nineteenth- and
    twentieth-century developments, see Gramit, D (2002) *Cultivating Music: The
    Aspirations, Interests and Limits of German Musical Culture 1779–1848*. Berkeley and
    London: California University Press.

7   The ideal of all-round musicianship, exercised at a high, often virtuosic degree of
    professionalism and skill, contained within itself vestiges of the Kapellmeister tradition,
    but on an altogether different level.

8   Beaumont, 2000, p.197

9   Schoenberg himself always acknowledged what Zemlinsky had shown (and in a sense
    'taught') him about Brahmsian technique and also about the creative reconciliation of
    Brahms and Wagner (see *inter alia* Schoenberg, 1975, p.80 and Schoenberg, Arnold
    (1988) *Arnold Schoenberg: Self-Portrait*, ed. Nuria Schoenberg Nono. Pacific Palisades:
    Belmont Music Publishers, p.72). And it is clear moreover that the classic essay 'Brahms
    the Progressive' (1947) must reflect more or less directly, at however remote a distance,
    their shared Brahmsian experiences and discussions of the 1890s – who can tell how
    many of the thoughts and insights it contains might not have originated with Zemlinsky?

10 Adorno, Theodor W (1972) *Ästhetische Theorie*, ed. Gretel Adorno and Rolf Tiedemann
    (Frankfurt a.M.: Suhrkamp, 1970; 2/1972); Eng. trans. Adorno (1984) *Aesthetic Theory*,
    trans. Christian Lenhardt. London and New York: Routledge and Kegan Paul (see above,
    n. 2).

11 „Aber sein Eklektizismus ist genial durch die Steigerung von Rezeptivität zu wahrhaft
    seismographischer Reaktionsfähigkeit all den Reizen gegenüber, von denen er sich
    überfluten lässt" (*Gesammelte Schriften*, 16: 354). I have used my own translation
    not because I have wilfully chosen to 'disregard' the excellent translation by Rodney
    Livingstone (1992), a book from which I have profited as everybody else has done, but
    rather because I believe it is absolutely in the spirit of Adorno's writing that every new
    author should engage afresh – tussle might be a better word – with his prose and ideas.

12 „Aber das Kraftfeld seines Werkes hat gerade darum seine Aktualität sich gerettet, weil
    die sogenannte große Entwicklungstendenz darüber hinwegging. Wie wenig andere
    Musik enthält die Zemlinskys Impulse in sich, welche das Neue in Bewegung brachten,
    die dann am Weg liegen blieben, deren Opfer aber etwas von dem Preis ausdrückt, der
    für den konsequenten Fortschritt zu zahlen war. Es ist der [Preis] der Prägung deutlicher,
    plastischer Einzelcharaktere" (*Gesammelte Schriften*, 16: 359).

13 Compare Adorno's view of the expressionist overlay which so often in Second Viennese

music tended to obscure the clear communication of distinct affects in its search for an intensity that was all-embracing – thus irresistible, and to that extent simplfying: 'The overall tendency of the Second Viennese School towards a making-essential (*zur Verwesentlichung*), [a tendency] which in so many respects involved also a certain simplification, went in Zemlinsky's case in the opposing direction – not away from communication, but towards it'. („Die Gesamtbewegung der neuen Wiener Schule zur Verwesentlichung, die in mancher Hinsicht stets auch Vereinfachung involvierte, verläuft bei Zemlinsky in umgekehrter Richtung, nicht weg von der Kommunikation sondern eher auf diese hin", *Gesammelte Schriften*, 16: 365).

14 „Wenn im Werk Schönbergs die divergentesten Impulse der Epoche sich durchdrangen und die Idee des konstruktiven Komponierens zeitigten, dann definiert Zemlinsky den musikalischen Bildungsbereich, in dem jene Impulse überhaupt einander vergleichbar wurden – außer Wagner und Brahms vor allem Mahler, Debussy und Schönberg. Das aber ist nicht als äußerliche Informiertheit des Komponisten über die wichtigsten sogennanten Zeitströmungen zu verstehen. Sondern *das Recht Zemlinskys, als den gehört zu werden, als welcher er seinen Wiener Freunden stets galt*, gründet darin, daß in seinem Werk bereits jene Kräfte aufs produktivste aneinander sich abarbeiten" (*Gesammelte Schriften*, 16: 357). Emphasis added.

15 Though we need to remember that neither he nor Schoenberg ever drew on folk materials as a formative and integrating component of modernism – as, say, Bartók and Janáček and Szymanowski all did during the interwar years. (Adorno, of course, had a generally negative view of the *völkisch* as a means to (self-)renewal in the quest for an authentically modern music – something which may be counted as one of his major blind spots.)

16 „Nicht umsonst klingt das Wort Synthese – Gegenbegriff von Manier wie von Eklektizismus – schal. Die Vermittlung des Divergenten will nur noch durch die Extreme hindurch, nicht durch den konzilianten Ausgleich geraten" (*Gesammelte Schriften*, 16: 351).

17 Tempo I = Allegretto (*Gemächlich, innig bewegt*); Tempo II = Allegro (*Viel bewegter als Tempo I, [lebhaft,] scharf rhythmisiert*). Fluctuations and transitions between these two 'structural tempi' (if they may be so called), as well as local inflections of them for dramatic or expressive reasons, exercise a striking degree of control over the flow of events, hence over the larger course of the movement. Not surprisingly, perhaps, Berg was using this technique of 'structural tempi' as early as the Piano Sonata Op. 1: see Jarman, D (1979) *The Music of Alban Berg*. London: Faber and Faber, pp.31–2 and 176.

18 Compare Schoenberg's stated view that 'the method by which balance is restored seems to me the real *idea* of a composition' (Schoenberg, 1975, p.123), and the measured but very telling commentary on Zemlinsky's Wunderhorn setting 'Das bucklichte Männlein' in Beaumont, 2000, pp.385–98 (see esp. pp.395–8).

19 Beaumont, 2000, p.421

20 Beaumont, 2000, pp.149–50 and 184 (and see above, n. 4)

21 Beaumont, 2000, pp.324–6

22 Beaumont, 2000, pp.401–2 and 410–13. He had conducted at the Krolloper under
    Klemperer (1927–1931) and taught at the Musikhochschule, while at the same time
    fulfilling conducting engagements elsewhere (1931–1933), before leaving Berlin for good
    in the early summer of 1933. He and Louise went to Vienna and resettled there after
    staying for most of the summer in Switzerland – where Zemlinsky then returned, to
    Zurich, for the premiere of *Der Kreidekreis*, at the beginning of October.

23 Beaumont, 2000, p.326. Zemlinsky is known to have attended the 1923 ISCM chamber
    music festival in Salzburg: his musical companions on that occasion were Berg and
    Heinrich Jalowetz (Beaumont, 2000, p.321 n.).

24 The Berg Op. 3, composed in 1910, was premiered in 1911 but not printed until December
    1920 (Vienna: Universal Edition). Publication of the Webern *Fünf Sätze* Op. 5 occurred
    in 1922, followed by the *Sechs Bagatellen* Op. 9 (with the famous prefatory note by
    Schoenberg) in 1924.

25 It is interesting to note the emergence and growth in the twentieth century of the
    sinfonietta as a genre in its own right: among those almost contemporaneous with
    Zemlinsky's are those of Janáček (1926), Prokofiev, Op. 48 (1929), Britten, Op. 1 (1932) and
    Roussel, Op. 52 (1934).

26 „Insgesamt hält sich die Sinfonietta im Umkreis jener [musikalischen] Produktion, da
    eine wissend gewordene Moderne mit den lange verschütteten Grundtypen der Wiener
    Klassik spielt, sie aus vollkommener Ungebundenheit wieder aufscheinen lässt, gleichsam
    [auch] zur eigenen Entlastung nutzt" (*Gesammelte Schriften*, 16: 363).

27 „Indessen hat Zemlinskys Sinfonietta nichts mit dem Neoklassizismus der
    Strawinskynachfolge zu tun. Weder borgt sie sich vergangene tektonische Statik aus, noch
    parodiert sie das Gewesene. Eher jongliert sie so schwerelos die überkommene Form, daß
    deren nachdrückliche Anspruch mit den lyrisch differenzierten Einzelereignissen gar
    nicht erst zusammenprallt. Zemlinskys Geschmack terminiert in einer Formgesinnung,
    die am liebsten die prohibitiven Schwierigkeiten von Symphonik heute durch Weglassen
    und Umgehung meistern möchte. Sie blickt nicht tierisch ernst nach rückwärts, entzieht
    sich aber andererseits doch dem Risiko neuer Durchkonstruktion aus symphonischem
    Geist" (*Gesammelte Schriften*, 16: 363).

28 It is surely no accident that such unobtrusively progressive scores as the Maeterlinck
    Songs, in their final 1921 version, and the *Symphonische Gesänge* should have been
    extended orchestral song cycles laid out on a symphonic scale. Here too the exemplary
    influence of late Mahler is evident, deriving in this instance from the model of *Das Lied
    von der Erde* (1908–9). The tradition also encompassed Zemlinsky's *Lyric Symphony*,
    Op. 18 (1922–3), premiered at the ISCM in Prague in 1924, and such works as Erwin
    Schulhoff's early 'vocal symphonies' *Landschaften*, Op. 26 and *Menschheit*, Op. 28.

29 Stravinsky, I and Craft, R (1968) *Dialogues and a Diary*, London: Faber and Faber, p.115.
    Stravinsky, I (1972) *Themes and Conclusions*. London: Faber and Faber, p.225.
    See also Pamela Tancsik and David Smith, in this volume, p.25 and n. 16, for another
    account of Stravinsky's reaction to this performance.

30 'I have admired the work of many conductors during my long career as a listener…'
declared *ex alto*, and with his customary un-self-doubting aplomb, Stravinsky the musical
arbiter (Stravinsky, 1972, p.225).

31 If music may legitimately be said to do cultural work, then compositions in their fully
realised form exist, and must exist, as a fusion of horizons between the texts (that is, the
scores) which are available in the *repertorium* or archive and the performing traditions
which interpret them and serve their best interests, aesthetically and expressively, by
representing them in sound to audiences in each successive generation.

32 'Certainly I lack that *je ne sais quoi* that one needs – today more than ever – to make one's
way. In such a crush it's no use just having elbows, one also has to know how to use them'
(quoted in Beaumont, 2000, p.351).

33 Berg died unexpectedly on 24 December 1935, having passed the 'fateful' date of the
23rd, which he had feared. His death came as a tremendous shock to all who knew him,
as Mathilde's had done just over twelve years previously. Instead of going to Barcelona
after Christmas to fulfil a series of conducting engagements, Zemlinsky stayed behind in
Vienna to begin work, more or less immediately, on a six-movement string quartet which
would memorialise his dead friend and also the musical concept of the 'Quartet Suite'
(Beaumont, 2000, pp.420–1). The Kolisch Quartet seem to have played the work privately
in America, but no public performance is known to have taken place before that given by
the LaSalle Quartet in 1967 (Beaumont, 2000, p.423 n.).

34 Schoenberg, 1975, pp.486–7 (see above, n. 4)

35 These were without doubt Schreker's greatest years, and the period of his finest
successes in the opera house, as chronicled by the acclaimed premieres of *Der ferne
Klang* (Frankfurt, 18 August 1912), *Die Gezeichneten* (Frankfurt, 25 April 1918) and *Der
Schatzgräber* (Frankfurt, 21 January 1920). He was by a considerable margin the most
performed and also by far the most successful serious opera composer of his era: see
inter alia Berg-Schoenberg (1987) *The Berg-Schoenberg Correspondence: Selected Letters*,
ed. Juliane Brand, Christopher Hailey and Donald Harris. New York and London: W.W.
Norton, p.368 and n. 2.

36 Newlin, D (1980) *Schoenberg Remembered: Diaries and Recollections (1938–76)*. New
York: Pendragon Press, p.294.

37 This much-debated phrase has a curious yet highly suggestive parallel in Adorno's
Aesthetic Theory, where the author is discussing the ability of 'authentic' artworks to
survive into the future, to remain not just neutrally 'available' but rather in a potentially
communicative state, rich in latent meaning, and awaiting a time when they will be able
to speak again with renewed vigour and intensity: 'Authentic art of the past may have to
hide its face for the time being; but it is not condemned for ever just because of that. Great
works are in a state of waiting (*Die großen Werke warten*). While their [full] metaphysical
meaning is gone they retain an element of their truth-content (*Wahrheitsgehalt*), an
element that is [nevertheless] difficult to identify. [And yet] it is that quality [of retaining
some truth] which enables them to remain articulate and communicative (*beredt* =
eloquent)' (*Ästhetische Theorie*, 1972, p.60).

38 Schoenberg, 1975, p.487

39 There is perhaps an indication here, however slight, that Schoenberg's partial return to
    tonality in certain of his later works, and the audible revisiting of his earlier manner, as
    seen, for example, in the 'expressionist' idiom of the String Trio, Op. 45 (1946) and the
    'Mahlerian' narrative breadth of *A Survivor from Warsaw*, Op. 46 (1947), may have had a
    more than purely musical origin.

40 To take just one example: the two movements of the Berg String Quartet Op. 3 show a
    number of possible, but in the end very uncertain, connections to formal archetypes and
    hidden tonal models; and the reason for this uncertainty is precisely the way the clear
    articulation of the form is at every point overlaid with thematic and textural elaboration
    of a complexity that takes on a life and a momentum of its own, and thus effectively
    shapes the dynamic and gestural course of the movement. See the remarks by Anthony
    Pople in Pople, A (ed.) (1997) *The Cambridge Companion to Berg*. Cambridge: Cambridge
    University Press, pp.76–82. Compare also Jarman (1979), pp.32–4 and 176–7.

41 Compare the apposite (and for the period perhaps rather surprising) remarks in
    Stravinsky, I (1959) *Conversations with Igor Stravinsky*, London: Faber and Faber, pp.28–9,
    on Beethoven's musical thought in relation to his use of the orchestra: 'It is not, generally,
    a good sign when the first thing we remark about a work is its instrumentation…
    Beethoven, the greatest orchestral master of all in our sense, is seldom praised for his
    instrumentation; his symphonies are too good music in every way, and the orchestra
    is too integral a part of them. How silly it sounds to say of the trio of the Scherzo of
    the Eighth Symphony: "what splendid instrumentation" – yet, what incomparable
    instrumental thought it is'.

42 Schoenberg, 1975, p.486

43 Schoenberg, 1975, p.487

44 Rainer Maria Rilke, *Sonette an Orpheus*, I, 9 (lines 1–8). Author's translation.

Antony Beaumont

Zemlinsky Editions
1993–2007

Introduction

ZEMLINSKY LEFT VIENNA AS a refugee in the autumn of 1938, making his way via Prague to the USA. Once he had found provisional quarters for his family, his housekeeper in Vienna arranged for furniture and personal effects to be dispatched to New York. The consignment, which included six cartons of manuscripts and personal papers, arrived in January 1939.

In 1962, twenty years after Zemlinsky's death, the Manhattan art dealer Otto Kallir negotiated the sale of all six cartons to the antiquarian Robert O. Lehman. Zemlinsky's widow, Louise, had struck the bargain on the understanding that she remained in possession of copyright, that the papers be conserved under appropriate climatic conditions, and that the autograph material be sorted and catalogued. In the event, Lehman was unable to fulfil the latter obligation, and in 1967 he donated the entire collection to The Library of Congress (LoC).[1] Lawrence Oncley set to work on compiling a comprehensive catalogue, which he published in 1975.[2] Led by Wayne Shirley, the LoC staff continued to revise and expand their finding list until August 1993.[3]

In the early 1970s, as Zemlinsky's music began to emerge from oblivion, his widow assigned the rights for the *Lieder* Opp. 22 and 27 to Mobart Music, Hillsdale.[4] The more substantial posthumous works[5] were entrusted to Universal Edition AG, Vienna (UE), who had published most of Zemlinsky's music between 1914 and 1935. While Mobart's publications were models of elegance and scholarship,[6] UE produced little more than stopgap editions – understandable, perhaps, considering that Zemlinsky was at the time all but unknown, and that the cost of publishing orchestral or choral works was far higher than anthologies of songs. Nevertheless, some of the misadventures were avoidable. The editor of the Fourth String Quartet, for example, seems to have known nothing of the autograph score at LoC, and worked instead from a set of handwritten parts at Harvard University; the editor of the Symphony in B-flat 'rationalized' Zemlinsky's notation, thereby expunging many subtleties of beaming and phrasing.

In 1987 Mrs Zemlinsky severed her ties with UE and signed an exclusive agreement with G. Ricordi & Co., Milan. Two years later, the contract was transferred to

Ricordi's German branch, in Munich.[7] First acquisitions, including the operas *Es war einmal...* and *Der Traumgörge*, the ballet *Ein Tanzpoem* and the *Drei Ballettstücke* drawn from it, were published in editions scarcely more reliable or pleasing to the eye than those of UE.

At the time, a well-known record company issued a disc with two Zemlinsky world premieres, *Ein Tanzpoem*, wrongly billed as '*Das gläserne Herz* (concert suite)', and the Symphony in D minor in a version that omitted the fourth movement (both works were subsequently published, intact and under their correct titles, by Ricordi – see 1.2.1. and 2.2.1. below). For lack of adequate research, it was contended that only the first forty bars of the Symphony's finale had survived.[8] In fact, the remainder, 361 bars in all, was present amongst the LoC holdings, but since the score lacked a title page, began *in medias res*, was written in an unidentified hand and on paper of an unusual format, Oncley had catalogued it as a separate item. The problem could perhaps have been solved in time for the recording, were it not that Mrs Zemlinsky, fearing theft or plagiarism, had insisted that access to all manuscript material be subject to her written permission. As encroaching blindness gradually isolated her from the outside world, the Zemlinsky Collection became all but inaccessible and research a game of hit-and-miss. Growing interest in the music was meanwhile nurtured by provisional transcripts, passed almost furtively from hand to hand.

The Zemlinsky Fonds[9] was founded in 1989 at the instigation of Mrs Zemlinsky, for the purpose of transferring her rights, royalties and other assets to an organisation in the public sector. The executive committee of the Fonds accepted my request to work on the Collection in search of material for a monograph, and later commissioned me to check for further publishable items. Armed with the necessary letter of authorisation, I set to work in Washington DC, later extending the quest to other locations in the USA, to Berlin, Copenhagen, London, Munich, Prague and Vienna. Much was found, much has meanwhile been published. The object of this paper is to review those publications, drawing attention to the problems that beset them, and indicating how those involved – the Munich branch of Ricordi, a completely reformed UE in Vienna, my co-editors and I – strove to find solutions.

I had scarcely begun to evaluate my findings at LoC before I received a reproving letter from Mrs Zemlinsky. The bone of contention was a projected Suite from the incidental music for Shakespeare's *Cymbeline* (1.1.2.). At my suggestion, Ricordi had requested permission to publish a *Bearbeitung* (adaptation) of the original theatre score. 'I cannot allow this,' she wrote, 'because I promised my husband that, as long as I lived, I would ensure that his works remained just as he left them.'[10] Behind the scenes the situation was explained to her, whereupon she withdrew her objection. Nevertheless, she remained wary of misrepresentation, refusing, for instance, to sanction a concert performance of *Ein Tanzpoem* in 1990 on grounds that it was a ballet and should therefore be performed only as such.[11]

On other occasions her actions seem to have been guided by emotion rather than reason. At a time when the opera *Der Zwerg* was known only to a handful of experts, what but emotion could have prompted her to sanction a 'new textual version'? She herself had sung the role of Second Lady-In-Waiting in the Prague production of 1926, and no doubt she recalled that the chief protagonist, a hideous and erotically hyperactive dwarf, had been interpreted in certain quarters as Zemlinsky's *alter ego*. Half a century later, she probably still winced at memories of ribald innuendoes and grotesque caricatures. On the proviso that the work be performed under a

different title, she gave the production team at Hamburg State Opera a free hand to abridge and rewrite as they saw fit.[12] Yet there can be little doubt that it had been Zemlinsky's explicit intention to bare his soul, that self-denigration was the very *raison d'être* for *Der Zwerg*. Those who knew the original libretto condemned the Hamburg version as a travesty. Nevertheless, *Der Geburtstag der Infantin*, as the work became known, held the stage for fifteen years, was widely performed, televised and recorded. The production did much to bring the music of Zemlinsky to a wider public. Since 1996, however, when an unabridged recording of the original score was released on CD, the Hamburg version has found its place in the limbo of music history.[13]

For no good reason at all, Mrs Zemlinsky also gave her *placet* to the plan for a *Traumgörge-Symphonie*, an adaptation of *Der Traumgörge* for two solo voices and large orchestra, reduced to a concert work comparable in size and scope to the *Lyric Symphony*.[14] If the idea had been to salvage the best of a work that was allegedly unstageable, it failed. When the Symphony finally reached the concert podium in Prague, Hamburg and elsewhere, in the mid-1990s, it transpired that the score was a mere pot-pourri, bereft of musical form or dramatic coherence.

A further project that required approval by Zemlinsky's widow was the completion of his last and arguably finest opera, *Der König Kandaules*. Crippled by two strokes and unable to complete the score himself, Zemlinsky had requested that the project be brought to a posthumous conclusion.[15] A few years after his death, Mrs Zemlinsky therefore approached a composer (who remains unidentified) in New York, but the initiative came to nothing. An old friend, the pianist Eduard Steuermann, warned her that this was no straightforward task, and that she shouldered a heavy burden of responsibility. Accordingly, when the son of a celebrated Viennese conductor offered his services (c.1971), she declined. In 1982 she contacted Friedrich Cerha, whose restoration work on Act III of Berg's *Lulu* had won international acclaim. Having studied photocopies of the autograph materials, Cerha concluded that the short-score was incomplete. Rather than compose pastiche Zemlinsky, he expressed his regrets and bowed out. Mrs Zemlinsky was led to believe that her Viennese 'friend' had absconded with some of the materials, at which stage, fearing further losses, she decided to close the LoC Collection to the general public. There was even talk of calling in the *Sureté* to interview the suspect at his Paris home. And yet, as Alfred Clayton noted in his dissertation of 1982, the short-score of *Kandaules* lay all the while complete and untouched at LoC, indeed the Collection also included the 'full score of most of Act I'.[16] My own, independent investigations, which confirmed Clayton's findings, prompted Peter Ruzicka and the Hamburg State Opera to commission me to reconstruct the short-score and complete the orchestration. I started work on the project in the autumn of 1991 and completed it two years later. One of Louise Zemlinsky's chief objects in founding the Fonds had been to ensure that, even if she should not live to see the day, *Kandaules* be completed. With the world premiere on 16 October 1996, almost exactly 125 years after Zemlinsky's birth and four years after her death, that goal was finally achieved.

Editorial policy

Schoenberg recalled admiringly that the young Zemlinsky was a *Schnellschreiber* (speed-writer) and a workaholic, who would practise for his next concert while waiting for the ink to dry on a freshly written sheet of manuscript paper.[17] As his career progressed, Zemlinsky rarely allowed the pace to slacken, composing, orchestrating and transcribing at breakneck speed, usually during intervals in a heavy conducting schedule.[18] Judging by the degree of error in his manuscript fair-copies[19] and his happy-go-lucky attitude towards proof-reading, such rapidity has proved in the long term to be less of an advantage.

While it was my concern to ensure that Zemlinsky's scores remained in principle 'just as he left them', it was clear that all the manuscripts at LoC needed judicious editing. But first it was necessary to decide which works were suitable for publication, and which would be better left to slumber in the archive. Fragments could be ruled out,[20] as could those compositions of which only fragments had survived. Other items, though complete, needed restoration on a larger scale than any latter-day editor could be expected to provide.

Having compiled a list of publishable works, the next step was to establish an editorial policy. Since there were no plans for a critical or complete edition, the publications were tailored primarily to practical needs. Therefore only a few of the works prepared under my supervision include a full-scale Editor's Report. Each score is prefaced instead by an Introduction, placing the work in its historical and biographical context before drawing attention to specific textual problems.

These were the salient points of editorial policy:

- The publications were to be presented bilingually in German and English
- German vocal underlay was to follow the spelling and hyphenation rules delineated in the 1989 edition of *Duden* (*Deutsches Universalwörterbuch*, Duden Verlag, Mannheim)
- Enharmonic notation of non-transposing instruments was to be retained, even if inappropriate (e.g. double-flats in harp notation)
- It was permissible to alter enharmonic notation of transposing instruments, where appropriate, for ease of reading
- It was permissible to add cautionary accidentals, where necessary, and to remove superfluous ones
- Complex or multiple slurs were to be left unaltered
- Editorial parentheses and/or footnotes were to be used to identify:
  a) additional conductor's markings in autograph scores
  b) editorial markings of phrasing and dynamics (though not of articulation)
  c) editorial tempo markings
- Editorial slurs were to be printed in scores – though not in individual instrumental parts – as dotted lines.

Zemlinsky's markings of articulation could be described as stenographic, and need to be interpreted in that spirit. Having defined the phrasing and articulation of any given figure or pattern of notes, he expects performers to adhere intuitively to the same scheme whenever it recurs. Subsequent recurrences are therefore often bereft of articulation markings. However, the absence of articulation can sometimes signal a departure from the established pattern. A case in point is the 'Birthday' theme at the opening of *Der Zwerg*. Zemlinsky notates the quaver-figure in bar 3 *without* accents, but at its first reiteration, in the last bar of this example, he notates it *with* accents:

Ex.1: *Der Zwerg*, opening bars (3 fg., 4 hr., vc., cb)

At first glance this looks like carelessness. Surely an editor should add the missing accents, publish and be damned? Yet the situation is not quite as straightforward as that. It could be argued, namely, that the omission of accents in bar 3 serves to place greater weight on the pitch-content of bars 4–5. If that was Zemlinsky's intention, then it is corroborated by the fact that he notates the quavers *consistently unaccented* over six separate staffs (two each for horns and bassoons, one each for cellos and basses). And since the second iteration of the 'Birthday' theme differs rhythmically from the first, if slightly, there is no reason for both to be identically phrased. In such an instance, rather than brandishing the red pencil, an editor should not intervene; rather than slavishly adding every marking that Zemlinsky appears to have omitted, such passages should be reproduced 'just as he left them'.

Obstacles

Pitch

In the earlier works, i.e. between 1890 and c.1903, the level of pitch error in Zemlinsky's manuscripts is often alarmingly high. Note-heads are not always precisely placed in relation to the staff, and chromatic passages often confusingly notated. Consequently, the degree of error in his first published works, notably the *Ländliche Tänze* Op. 1 and the *Clarinet Trio* Op. 3, is also high. As from 1904, when he began work on *Der Traumgörge*, the situation improves. Pitch errors are fewer and further between, and occur as often as not in passages for transposing instruments. Occasional confusion also arises in passages where he failed to take account of the prevailing key signature (e.g. *Der Zwerg*, new edition p. 221 et seq., where, in a context of F minor, the autograph frequently reads G-flat instead of G-natural).

Modes of execution

When writing for woodwind and brass, Zemlinsky applies the term *Flatterzunge* indiscriminately to double-tonguing ('Zungenschlag') and genuine flutter-tonguing. As a rule, where repeated notes are written out in full, double-tonguing is intended; passages of single notes notated with tremolo strokes imply true flutter-tonguing.

A further idiosyncrasy of Zemlinsky's is his habit of notating *col legno* passages with staccato dots. Maybe the intention was to differentiate between *battuto* and *arcato* playing, but the latter effect – to the best of my knowledge – never occurs in his music, besides which his use of staccato dots is inconsistent. The length of a *col legno battuto* note cannot be influenced by the performer – except, of course, on an open string. Hence, strictly speaking, the dots are superfluous.

Dynamics

Particularly in larger scores, dynamic markings are frequently inconsistent or incomplete. Rarely, for instance, does Zemlinsky notate a crescendo uniformly in all voices. Some voices are marked '*cresc.*', others bear crescendo forks, and these often diverge in length and alignment from one staff to the next; some voices are not marked at all. The markings do not always indicate where a crescendo should end, or the dynamic level at which it should reach its apex. The sequel to a Zemlinskian crescendo is often an abrupt drop in dynamic, whereby some instruments pause, then re-enter at a lower dynamic level. In such cases, the new dynamic is often unspecified. Clarification is also needed in passages marked '*espr.*', where the dynamic level is often omitted.

Musical notation and calligraphy

Zemlinsky's musical hand is generally clear, but diminutive to the extent that accidentals often need to be verified under magnification. Where minims are seated over leger lines, particular care is needed, for Zemlinsky's minims are often rhomboids rather than circles (cf. contrabass line, Example 2), and it is easy to misread the lower horizontal of a rhomboid minim as an extra leger line.[21]

Ex. 2: *Die Seejungfrau*, third movement, bar 45, strings

There is another, more intriguing point to Example 2. At a cursory glance, the first pitch in Violin I reads as b". Under magnification, however, it stands revealed as a", preceded by a (superfluous and slightly misplaced) natural and topped by an accent. Not surprisingly, that pitch, even though it stands prominently in the melodic line, and despite being doubled at the correct pitch by oboes and clarinets, has been misread ever since the work was revived in 1984.

Zemlinsky's *Kurrentschrift*, the standard script in Austria and Germany from the middle of the 19th century until its abolition by the National Socialist regime in 1941, is a more formidable obstacle than anything in the realm of musical notation. Today, as the last generation schooled in *Kurrentschrift* passes on, the script has become the domain of specialists. Earlier versions of the LoC Special Guide included a setting of a poem by Franz Werfel, listed (nonsensically) as 'Ahnung Beatriens':

Ex. 3: LoC 23/8, title at head of opening page

The correct reading is 'Ahnung Beatricens' ('Beatricens' being the German genitive of the Italian 'Beatrice'), i.e. 'Intimation of Beatrice'. The *Schnellschreiber* elides the c and e to the point of near-illegibility. Where a word is uncommon, as here, misreadings are forgivable. Where the illegible word appears to be in standard usage, an intelligent guess usually misses the mark. Even Zemlinsky's friends and contemporaries sometimes jumped to false conclusions:

a. original MS (1904)

b. copyist's score, Vienna
Hofoper (1906–07)

c. published vocal score
(Bodanzky, 1906–07)

d. Ricordi edition
(2003–07)

Ex. 4: *Der Traumgörge*, act I, scene iv, bar 437, timpani

Not only the unidentified copyist at the Vienna Hofoper, but also Arthur Bodanzky, a pupil and close friend of Zemlinsky, read the first word as 'Mässig', implying that this bar, which intersects a tutti passage marked 'Äußerst lebhaft' (extremely animated), should be played at a moderate tempo.[22] Zemlinsky's intention was that the timpani play powerfully ('wuchtig'), while retaining the rapid tempo: quite the opposite effect.

List of edited works

1. First editions of completed compositions

1.1. Stage

1.1.1. *Ein Lichtstrahl* mime-drama with piano

Comp. 1901. MS sources: holograph score (Vienna version, 1901) LoC[23] 9/20; copyists's score with two holograph additions (Leipzig version, *c*.1902) LoC 9/21. Sy. 5007

Since the Vienna and Leipzig versions diverge quite radically, the published edition includes both.

1.1.2. Incidental music for Shakespeare's *Cymbeline*[24]

Comp. 1913–15. MS source: holograph full score, LoC 16/14. Sy. 5041

The full score has been checked, presumably by a member of the music staff at the Mannheim Nationaltheater, where *Cymbeline* was due to be staged in the 1914–15 season. Uncertain pitches are marked with a pencilled 'x', and the closing page is marked: 'x Bitte Herrn Zemlinsky fragen' ('Please ask Mr Zemlinsky').

1.2. Orchestral

1.2.1. Symphony in D minor

Comp. 1892–3. MS sources: copyists's full score (movts. 1, 2 and 3, and the first 45 bars of movt. 4); holograph full score (movt. 4, from bar 41) LoC 1/13. Sy. 5013. See also 2.2.1.

The copied portions of the score are distressingly erratic. Since no further sources were available for comparison, editorial corrections were founded entirely on common-sense.

1.3. Vocal

1.3.1. *Waldgespräch* Ballad for soprano, two horns, harp and strings

Comp. 1895–6. MS source: holograph full score, LoC 4/5–6. Sy. 5027

In the autograph score, three tempo markings have been corrected and two instrumental entries have been deleted, presumably during rehearsal. Further emendations to the score suggest that Zemlinsky subsequently contemplated a version with four horns.

1.3.2. *Maiblumen blühten überall* for soprano and string sextet

Comp. 1899. MS source: holograph full score (incomplete) LoC 26/12. Sy. 5009

Viola II does not enter until bar 42, and the absence of space for a sixth staff in the opening accolades suggests that the work was originally envisaged as a quintet with two cellos. The autograph score includes 43 bars of a *II. Theil*, which breaks off in mid-phrase at the end of the 13th folio. In accordance with the policy outlined above, this fragment remains unpublished.

In the Introduction to the published score, I asserted that 'no sketches or other related material have survived'. Since then, an eight-bar sketch for the opening of the second movement has come to light, written on the verso of a sketch for the orchestral Prelude to the opera *Es war einmal...*

According to the date entered in the autograph score of the latter, it was completed in March 1899. Hence *Maiblumen* should be dated to the same period, not to 1903, as I had previously surmised.

The work is also published in an adaptation for string orchestra (see 5.3.2)

1.3.3. *Minnelied* for TTBB chorus, 2 flutes, 2 horns and harp

Comp. *c.*1895. MS source: holograph sketch and full score, LoC 3/17 and 3/18. Sy. 5024

As published, the edition includes a rehearsal score with piano, transcribed by the editor.

1.3.4. Hochzeitsgesang (*Baruch aba; Mi adir*) motet for cantor, SATB chorus and organ

Comp. 1896. MS source: holograph full score, LoC 3/7. Sy. 5025

This is Zemlinsky's only surviving setting of a text from the Hebrew liturgy. The main editorial problem was the absence of word underlay. The editor's putative underlay was corrected with the aid of Rabbi Benyamin Barslai (Bremen).

1.3.5. Zwei Gedichte for SATB chorus and string orchestra (see also 4.3.1.)

Comp. 1896. MS sources: sketches and holograph full score, LoC 7/1. Sy. 5008

The second piece, *Geheimnis*, which survives only in short-score format, was transcribed for string orchestra by the editor (see 5.3.1.).

1.3.6. Frühlingsbegräbnis for soprano and baritone soli, chorus and large orchestra

Comp. April–July 1896; orch. *c.*1897; rev. and re-orch. *c.*1903. MS sources: a) original version: holograph sketches and short score LoC 6/7; copyist's vocal score LoC 6/7; full score LoC 6/8; vocal score and complete performing materials: Gesellschaft der Musikfreunde, Vienna; b) revised version: sketches LoC 7/9; holograph full score LoC 7/10. Sy. 5010

The Ricordi full-score follows the text of LoC 7/10. The published vocal score, while largely following LoC 6/7, was adapted to the variants of the revised version.

Compared with the original, the revised version includes four extra bars before bar 102, two extra bars before bar 137, two extra bars before bar 278 and a fugato of twenty-two bars in the 'storm' chorus. There are numerous harmonic modifications, the baritone aria (bars 219–278) is partly rewritten; six bars are cut before bar 450 and the rest of the passage is substantially modified; the orchestral peroration (from bar 456) is shortened from forty-one to twenty bars and partly rewritten. Judging by the eminently playable piano writing of his short-score, Zemlinsky may originally have conceived the work with piano accompaniment. Nevertheless the autograph includes numerous notes for orchestration. The first orchestral version is scored for 3(picc.)-2-2-2; 4-2-3-1; timp., perc., harp and strings. Zemlinsky later expanded the woodwind from double to triple, adding an English horn and a bass clarinet, a third trumpet and a second harp, and altered numerous details of phrasing, articulation and instrumental texture. Two unusual features: a) contrary to his generally parsimonious use of manuscript paper, here Zemlinsky writes only five bars per page; b) the chorus part, from bar 42, is entered into the score one bar too soon and remains out of synchronisation with the orchestra for eleven bars. From a) it can be inferred that the score was written for a fee, payable per page;[25] b) implies that the score was never used in performance (an error of such magnitude would have been corrected in rehearsal). None of Zemlinsky's orchestral music appeared in print before 1914,[26] but in the spring of 1903 he entered into negotiations with the Süddeutsche Musikverlag in Strasbourg to publish the *Drei Ballettstücke*, composed in 1901–2.[27] It could be postulated that the revised version of *Frühlingsbegräbnis* was commissioned by the same publisher, in which case it could be dated to the same period.

1.3.7. *Aurikelchen* for female voices (SSA)

Comp. unknown. MS sources: holograph score. Sy. 5023

In lieu of editorial comment, the work was published with a complete facsimile of the autograph score.

1.3.8. Posthumous Songs

Comp. 1889–1939. MS sources: diverse locations, mostly LoC. Sy. 5002

Many of these thirty-nine songs testify to Zemlinsky's love of harmonic experiment. Hence, the most significant area of editorial intervention was the identification and clarification of pitches. Specific problems:

In der Sonnengasse: in the autograph, a large ink-stain obliterates several bars of the piano part. The content was reconstructed by shining a powerful torchlight on the paper (not normally recommended!) and reading it from the verso side.

Fünf Dehmel-Lieder (1907). Though probably conceived as a cycle, the intended performing order is uncertain. The autograph fair copy of 'Vorspiel' follows (on the same page) directly after 'Ansturm'; 'Letzte Bitte' and 'Auf See' survive only as rough drafts. There also exists a draft version of 'Vorspiel', and a further fragment of the same song is sketched out beneath the draft of 'Letzte Bitte'. 'Stromüber' is preserved as a fair copy with a separate title page. The manuscripts of 'Ansturm' and 'Stromüber' bear indications for the engraver, implying that Zemlinsky may at some stage have intended to publish at least these two songs.

1.4. Chamber

1.4.1. String Quartet in E minor

Comp. *c*.1892–3. MS sources: holograph score, hand-copied parts with pencilled alterations LoC 3/10–11. Sy. 5019. Edited in collaboration with Werner Loll.

1.4.2. Three Pieces for Cello and Piano

Comp. 1890. MS source: holograph score, Archive of Gesellschaft der Musikfreunde in Wien. Sy. 5046

1.4.3. Cello Sonata in A minor

Comp. 1894. MS sources: holograph score and handwritten cello part (copyist unidentified), owner unknown. Sy. 5045

I was able to inspect the original MS for forty minutes before it was auctioned at Sotheby's in December 2005. Because of the large number of dubious and putative readings in all three movements, this edition is supported by a full Editor's Report.

1.4.4. Two Movements for String Quintet (1894–6)

Comp. 1894 and 1896. MS sources: holograph scores LoC 3/14 and LoC 4/7. Sy. 5014. Edited in collaboration with Werner Loll.

The first source includes Zemlinsky's final draft of the opening Allegro and his preliminary sketches for the succeeding movements.[28] The second is a fair copy of the Prestissimo finale. Legibility is hampered in the former by ink-stains and smudges. There are also several deletions, the most substantial passage (eleven bars) originally placed between bars 204–205.

1.4.5. Two Movements for String Quartet (1927)

Comp. 1927. MS source: holograph score LoC 20/4. Sy. 5015. Edited in collaboration with Werner Loll.

Apart from the two published movements, the manuscript includes four undated fragments, not included in the edition.[29] The work, designated on the title page as *IV. Quartett* dates from the summer of 1927, when the composer was on holiday in the Salzkammergut. The fact that Zemlinsky composed a six-movement work bearing the same title in 1936 implies that he abandoned all thought of completing or publishing the earlier work.

A problem of transcription arises in the viola, bars 6–9 of the second movement:

In passages related to this idea (violin I, bar 13–14, cello bar 124–6), the texture is monodic, suggesting that these bars should follow suit. The edition includes both the variants, viola solo and viola with cello (the latter as an *ossia*). The lower line could conceivably be read in the tenor clef, rather than bass, but the orthography (A-natural followed by F-flat) seems unlikely, and the combination cacophonous in the extreme.

1.4.6. Selected piano pieces.

Comp. 1892–1901. Sources: diverse, partly handwritten (holograph scores), partly drawn from early printed editions, LoC and private collections. Sy. 5016

Specific problems:

Four Ballads. Bar 91–3: '2T.', enclosed within a large caret sign, is added in pencil at the end of bar 91, indicating the intention to add two further bars. Using bars 33–34 as a model, I have incorporated a possible realisation of the composer's shorthand, printed in cue-sized notes.

2. Reconstructions of incomplete or fragmentary works

2.1. Stage

2.1.1. *Der König Kandaules*

Comp. 1935–8. MS sources: sketches, short-score, fragmentary holograph full score (846 bars) LoC 188–192. Sy. 5012

2.2. Orchestral

2.2.1. Symphony in D minor, last movement

see 1.2.1. above. The copyist's score continues up to bar 45, but the last page (starting at bar 40) contains only the flute and oboe parts. Since bar 40 is entirely blank, and the surviving pages of Zemlinsky's holograph score begin at bar 41, the missing bar had to be inferred from the parallel passage later in the movement, at bar 283.

2.3. Vocal

2.3.1. *Zwei Gesänge* for baritone and orchestra

Comp. 1900–1. MS source: holograph short-score LoC 14/11. Sy. 5037

Since the last folio of the first song, 'Der alte Garten', has lost its top left-hand corner, the vocal line and upper orchestral voices in bar 61 are putative. Zemlinsky did not compose bars 213–6 of the second song, 'Erdeinsamkeit', but indicated with a caret sign and the words '4 Takte' his intention to add them later.

2.4. Chamber

2.4.1. Quartet for clarinet and strings

Comp. 1938–9. MS sources: numerous holograph fragments LoC 24/3–4. Sy. 5042

The publication juxtaposes the two most extensive fragments, the first composed in Vienna during the summer of 1938, the second in New York the following January.

3. Corrected editions of works in print

3.1. Stage

3.1.1. *Der Traumgörge*

Comp. 1904–6. MS sources: copyist's full score ÖNB (Austrian State Library, Vienna)[30], holograph sketches and full score LoC 12/9, 13 and 14/1–6. Published sources: libretto and vocal score (three discrepant editions), Karczag und Wallner, Vienna, 1906 and 1907. Sy. 5011

In preparation. Expected publishing date: autumn 2007.

3.1.2. *Der Zwerg*

Comp. 1919–21. MS source: holograph full score LoC 20/1. Published sources: vocal score, 1921, publishers' hire score UE 6630 and libretto, 1922. UE 17571

A remark on the title page of the autograph score – 'Original score / fully corrected & retouched / (only this copy is correct)' – went for many years unnoticed. Zemlinsky's remark must be understood as referring primarily to his cuts and retouchings. From an editorial point of view, in a score as complex as this, these are merely the tip of the iceberg.

3.2. Orchestral

3.2.1. *Lyric Symphony* Op. 18

Comp. 1922–3. MS sources: holograph full score ÖNB, short-score LoC 20/2. Published sources: vocal score, 1923; orchestral score, 1926. UE 3273

While retaining the engraved image of the original 1925 score, the new edition provides a systematically correlated and corrected reading of Zemlinsky's text. The simultaneous publication of new orchestral materials (UE 30 149) will satisfy those demands for legibility and accuracy which hitherto remained unfulfilled. Since the autograph score is itself by no means free of error, reference has also been made to the published vocal score, a cyclostyled errata list by Heinrch Jalowetz (UE), the manuscript short score (LoC) and corrections entered by Zemlinsky into his personal copy of the printed score (Moldenhauer Collection, Harvard University).

3.2.2. *Sinfonietta* Op. 23

Comp. 1934. MS sources: holograph full score ÖNB, sketches LoC 23/5. Published source: UE full score 10.287. UE 31926

Before publication of the hand-copied hire score in 1935 (UE 10287), both Jalowetz and Zemlinsky conducted the *Sinfonietta* from the original manuscript. A number of corrections and retouchings were pencilled into this score, most of which were later incorporated into the hire score; a few subsequent amendments were evidently passed on directly to the copyist. Unfortunately the master set of orchestral parts – and hence all performing materials in circulation since 1945 – were only partially updated. The new edition correlates the text of the autograph with both sets of revisions and rectifies a few slips of the composer's pen. With the simultaneous publication of new orchestral parts (UE 32509), problems of consistency and accuracy have been eliminated.

4. Miscellanea and work in progress

4.1. Stage

4.1.1. *Sarema*, Prelude

Comp. 1893–5. MS sources: holograph full score, Bavarian State Library, Munich. Sy. 5006

4.1.2. *Es war einmal...*, Prelude

Comp. 1897–9. MS sources: copyist's full score ÖNB, holograph full score LoC 9/3–5. Sy. 5038

4.1.3. *Es war einmal...*, vocal score of Urtext version

Comp. 1897–9. MS sources: copyist's full score ÖNB, holograph full score LoC 9/3–5, cyclostyled vocal score British Library, revised cyclostyled vocal score ÖNB.

In preparation. This is the first stage of a project to publish a new, two-volume edition (including full score and performing materials) of the complete opera. Vol. I: preferred reading, corresponding to the version conducted by Mahler at the Vienna Hofoper; Vol. II: variants and appendices, consisting of original versions of scenes altered at Mahler's behest, and scenes added by Zemlinsky for the 1912 productions in Mannheim and Prague.

4.1.4. *Eine florentinische Tragödie*

Comp. 1915–18. MS sources: holograph score LoC 18/6–7, orchestral material, part printed, part handwritten, with Zemlinsky's holograph corrections Archive of the National Theater, Prague. Published sources: publisher's hire score UE 5663.

In preparation.

4.2. Orchestral

4.2.1. Symphony in B-flat major. Unpublished

Comp. 1897. MS source: holograph score LoC 7/8–9.

Provisionally corrected edition, prepared for my CD recording in January 2001.

4.2.2. *Die Seejungfrau*

Comp. 1902–3. MS sources: holograph score of first movt. ÖNB; holograph score of second and third movts. LoC 12/2–4.

In preparation.

4.3. Vocal

4.3.1. Posthumous Songs, revised, expanded and newly engraved

In preparation

The new edition will include several items that were previously overlooked or undiscovered.

4.4. Chamber

4.4.1. Albumleaf on B-A-C-H (medium unspecified)

Comp. 1924. MS source: Gonville and Caius College, Cambridge (library)

In preparation

5. *Transcriptions and orchestrations*

5.1. Stage

5.1.1. *Circe*

Comp. 1939. MS source: holograph sketches and short-score fragment LoC 25/5–8 and 25/10. Unpublished.

Lied der Circe, transcription for voice and piano. To be included in the revised edition of the Posthumous Songs.

5.2. Orchestral

5.2.1. Suite from the music for Shakespeare's *Cymbeline*. Sy. 5028

5.3. Vocal

5.3.1. 'Geheimnis' (No. 2 of *Zwei Gedichte*) transcription for string orchestra. Sy. 5008.

5.3.2. *Maiblumen blühten überall* transcription for string orchestra. Sy. 5032

Notes

1 Other items, notably the autograph score of Psalm 13, were deposited in the Toscanini Memorial Archives at New York Public Library.

2 Oncley, Lawrence A (1975) *The published works of Alexander Zemlinsky*, diss., University of Indiana.
   Oncley, Lawrence A (1977) 'The Works of Alexander Zemlinsky: A Chronological List', *MLA Notes*, 34, December 1977, pp.291–302.

3 The finding list, incorporated in LoC's *Guide to Special Collections* series, and dated '1992 (rev. 8/93)', can be consulted online under http://hdl.loc.gov/loc.music/eadmus.mu2005. wp.0043.pdf

4 Now affiliated to Boelke-Bomart Music Publishers, Englewood NJ. Mobart published the *Sechs Gesänge* Op. 22 in 1977 together with two songs without opus number, 'Ahnung Beatricens' and 'Das bucklichte Männlein'; the *Zwölf Gesänge* Op. 27 followed in 1978.

5 Psalm 13 (1971), String Quartet no. 4 (1974), Symphony in B- flat (1977) and *Die Seejungfrau* (1984). Universal also published three chamber works, the two late 'school pieces' 'Hunting piece' (1977) and 'Humoreske' (1978), and the Serenade for violin and piano (1984).

6 Both volumes were edited (anonymously) by Jacques-Louis Monod.

7 G. Ricordi & Co. Bühnen- und Musikverlag, Munich.

8 Marco Polo 8.223166 (Czecho-Slovak Radio Symphony Orchestra conducted by Ludovit Rajter), recorded in 1989 and reissued in 2003 (unaltered) on Naxos 8.557008. The

booklet note makes no mention of the fourth movement. Correspondence found in Mrs Zemlinsky's posthumous papers reveals that the record company had considered commissioning a finale based on the 40-bar fragment.

9 Full title: Alexander Zemlinsky Fonds bei der Gesellschaft der Musikfreunde in Wien.

10 'Ich kann die Bewilligung [...] nicht geben, da ich meinem Mann versprochen habe, dass ich mich mein ganzes Leben dafuer einsetzen werde, dass sein Werk so verbleibt, wie er es hinterlassen hat.' Letter from Louise Zemlinsky to the author, New York, 8 April 1991.

11 *Ein Tanzpoem* finally reached the concert-hall – to splendid effect – in Cologne on 20 October 1996.

12 The opera was premiered in Hamburg on 20 September 1981 under the title *Der Geburtstag der Infantin.*

13 Cologne Philharmonic (Gürzenich-Orchester) conducted by James Conlon, EMI 7243 5 66248 2 5.

14 *Traumgörge-Symphonie* for soprano and tenor solo, realization by Frank Maus, idea by Gerd Albrecht.

15 For a detailed German-language account of the *Kandaules* project, the reader is referred to Antony Beaumont, 'Zemlinsky: *Der König Kandaules*: Arbeitsbericht', in *Das Fragment im (Musik-)Theater. Zufall und/oder Notwendigkeit?* Vorträge und Gespräche des Salzburger Symposiums 2002. Wort und Musik, Salzburger akademische Beiträge, 55, Anif/Salzburg 2005, pp.111–34.

16 Clayton, Alfred (1982) *The Operas of Alexander Zemlinsky*, diss., Cambridge, p.363n. According to Louise Zemlinsky, her husband had completed the orchestral score up to the end of Act II.

17 Schönberg, Arnold (1976) 'Herz und Hirn in der Musik', *Stil und Gedanke. Aufsätze zur Musik*, Frankfurt a.M., p.105.

18 During the summer of 1921, Zemlinsky produced 234 pages of full score for *Der Zwerg* in the space of two months: an average of over five pages per day.

19 The list of errata in the autograph full-score of *Die Seejungfrau*, as compiled by Keith Rooke, fills twenty closely spaced pages (*Alexander Zemlinsky's symphonic Poem: 'The Mermaid'. An identification and historical evaluation.* diss., Manchester, 1981).

20 An exception was made in the case of the Clarinet Quartet (see 2.4.1.).

21 This also occurs with smaller note-values, e.g. in the UE study score of String Quartet No. 3 Op. 19, at one bar before fig. 4, where in his personal copy (Moldenhauer Archive, Harvard University) Zemlinsky corrects the d''' in Violin 1 to b''.

22 In all fairness to Bodanzky, one cannot rule out the possibility that he worked from the copyist's score, rather than from the autograph.

23 LoC x/x = The Library of Congress, Alexander von Zemlinsky Collection, box number/ file number. The entire collection is also preserved on microfilm. Reel numbers in the Library's finding list are still subject to sporadic updates.

24 See also 4.2.1.

25 André Previn, in conversation with the author, pointed out that, to this day, Hollywood

film composers calculate their fees on a similar basis (four bars per page).

26 The work published in 1914 was Psalm 23 Op. 13.

27 cf. Weber, Horst (ed.) (1996) *Zemlinskys Briefwechsel mit Schönberg, Webern, Berg und Schreker*, Briefwechsel der Wiener Schule i, Darmstadt, p.43. The co-operation with the Süddeutsche Musikverlag never materialized, and the *Drei Ballettstücke* were first published in 1994 by G. Ricordi, Munich.

28 Adagio, A-flat major, 62 bars; Scherzoso, C major, 9 bars; Finale, D major, 27 bars.

29 Intermezzo (Allegro molto, 131 bars) and Trio (44 bars, followed by four bars' varied reprise of the Allegro), Theme with Variations (28 bars), Allegro moderato e appassionato (64 bars) and Allegro con fuoco (86 bars).

30 Also original performing materials.

Christopher Dromey

Zemlinsky's Surface Structures: Maiblumen blühten überall and the String Sextet Genre

BRAHMS'S PAIR OF STRING sextets (Opp. 18, 36) heralded a heyday for the medium. A spate of sextets was written in their aftermath, most notably by Dvořák, Tchaikovsky and Schoenberg, but they did not secure a legacy robust enough to resist the modern characterisation of the sextet as an inferior cousin to the string quartet. Ironically, the latest of these works, Schoenberg's famous *Verklärte Nacht*, Op. 4, did most to impair the generic autonomy of its medium. Schoenberg forever altered the string sextet's terms of reference. Notwithstanding his *fin de siècle* harmonies – cause of the most immediate scandal – discussion of musical and extramusical structures in the work has since cast a greater shadow over the putative string sextet genre. Carl Dahlhaus's defence of programme music is typical:

> [T]he formal rigour [of *Verklärte Nacht*] seems like a concession to the tradition of the string quartet, of which the string sextet represents a variation in scoring rather than constituting a genre of its own – [but] it is also a piece of programme music; and the programme... can easily be read in the music, at least in its outlines.... The prejudice that regards the programmatic tendency as nothing but an attempt to shore up fragile musical forms with extramusical arguments, and, by means of literary associations, to create a (perhaps deceptive) impression of unity where musically there is none, is thus revealed as fallacious.[1]

Pitting the string quartet against new or reborn configurations such as the string sextet is a favourite theme of commentators during an era in which, actually, the representation and definition of chamber music was fundamentally changed. From Stravinsky's apathy for the string quartet, to the rise of mixed ensembles, especially the progenies of Schoenberg's *Pierrot lunaire*, Op. 21, the quartet's stock plummeted.

With its 'tradition' challenged, can the quartet really be an adequate benchmark by which to judge the string sextet? Certainly the characteristics which fashioned its heritage appear unsuited to the task. To submit to the assumed supremacy of the quartet is to discount that its celebrated blend of intimacy, discursiveness and dramaticism does not sit easily with the newer, larger medium. When Schoenberg and Tchaikovsky (*Souvenir de Florence*, Op. 70) made transcriptions for string orchestra which have proved more popular than their original sextets, they shifted perceptions of the genre further still from the intimate world of the quartet but eclipsed the genre in the process; such blurring of the boundaries of chamber music defies the arbitrary limits on it some have tried to impose.[2] Similarly, for Dahlhaus, *Verklärte Nacht* confounds critics of programme music because its 'closed musical form' (purported to derive from the quartet) is a counterbalance to its extramusical narrative. Case-specific, his structuralist argument precludes a string sextet genre and also appears to sideline the surface gestures that compose Schoenberg's music-dramatic analogue.

Still, the dilemma for proponents of such a genre is that according to current thinking, *Verklärte Nacht* is so atypical of other string sextets that it ruptures its nineteenth-century lineage. Dahlhaus and others were unaware of another string sextet inspired, like Schoenberg's, by the poetry of Richard Dehmel. Zemlinsky's incomplete setting of 'Die Magd' (*The Maid*) was published in 1997 under the title of the poem's first line, *Maiblumen blühten überall* ('Maybuds blossomed all around').[3] In *Maiblumen*, Dehmel's words are sung by a soprano, though curiously her role is minor: she never shares in the swooning opening melody of the first viola, or in the related counter-melody of the first cello whose principal motif is imitated by every other instrument thereafter, even the briefly heard second viola (Ex. 1). Marginalised, her belated entry (bar 48) piggybacks on the chromatic tail of the extended instrumental introduction, in the same way that the thematic character of the opening recedes from bar 8 onwards.[4] Nevertheless, *Maiblumen* is regarded at best as a footnote to discussion of Schoenberg's sextet, and when Zemlinsky scholars still grapple with basic uncertainties such as *Maiblumen*'s date, while others appear to dismiss the concept of a string sextet genre altogether, the disparity is clear.

In his chronicle of Zemlinsky's chamber music, Werner Loll was the first to commentate on *Maiblumen*. However, his suggestion that the piece was probably contemporaneous with another then unpublished fragment for string sextet sketched in 1899 is largely speculative.[5] Antony Beaumont was persuaded that *Maiblumen* was composed much later by Zemlinsky's reaction to the 1902 premiere of *Verklärte Nacht*, specifically his plea to Schoenberg to 'revise... and disseminate' the work.[6] That Karl Weigl, Zemlinsky's former pupil, set 'Ein Stelldichein' (Dehmel again) in 1903 for the same voice-and-sextet line-up encourages the idea of a lineage inspired, rather than interrupted, by Schoenberg. But the recent discovery of a *Maiblumen* sketch on the reverse of another for the prelude to *Es war einmal...* (dated March 1898) means Zemlinsky's sextet was almost certainly written during that year.[7] His fateful 'Alma crisis' therefore had no bearing on his abandonment of *Maiblumen*,[8] yet it is possible that unfavourable comparison with Schoenberg led the rarely self-assured Zemlinsky to bow out gracefully.

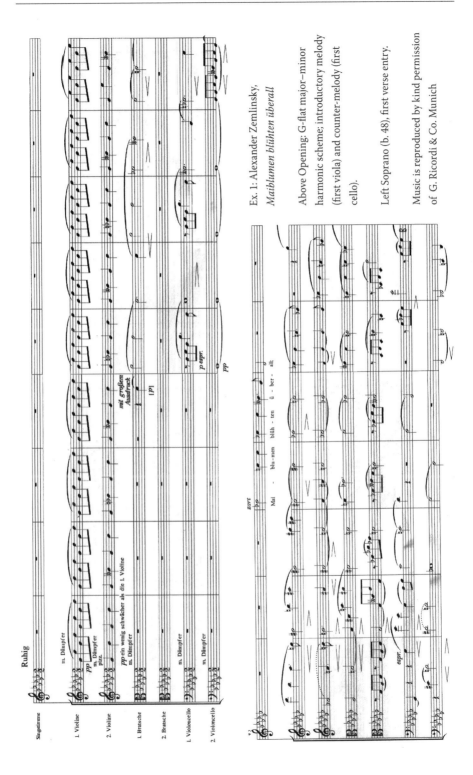

Ex. 1: Alexander Zemlinsky, *Maiblumen blühten überall*

Above Opening: G-flat major–minor harmonic scheme; introductory melody (first viola) and counter-melody (first cello).

Left Soprano (b. 48), first verse entry.

Music is reproduced by kind permission of G. Ricordi & Co. Munich

Ex. 2: *Maiblumen blühten überall*, second verse.

Over a century later, *Maiblumen* is no longer dormant. Already recorded three times since it was published, its medium, date, and compositional design change our understanding of the string sextet genre. Loll first drew attention to *Maiblumen*'s 'web of motivic references' (*Netz motivischer Bezüge*) but in trying to rationalise the structure of a work that is incomplete, his proposal of sonata form as Zemlinsky's compositional model is tenuous.[9] Although this aptly consigns the first-verse soprano entry to a bridge passage, the material which introduces Dehmel's second stanza is too clearly demarcated and different in character to correspond (Ex. 2). The soprano's ascending scale, now in the enharmonic F-sharp minor, is more expansive and coherent than before, but its repetitive rhythms expose a fragmentary texture beneath: the sextet's suddenly disruptive articulation foretells the drama which will unfold. Beaumont stops short of identifying a conventional musical structure but comments that the two verses form a 'thematically integrated unit'.[10] Corresponding enharmonically, their harmonic-structural scheme certainly appears to protract the same major/minor device which introduced *Maiblumen*. But the music's cogent synthesis into a prevailing G-flat/F-sharp tonal model is unrealistic, just as the motivic play which characterises the opening and the start of each verse foils a genuinely thematic style. This is because Zemlinsky consistently thwarts the continuity of the major/minor system by drawing on modified diminished and minor harmonies – their coincidence with denser and more contrasting moments of articulation in the string sextet is what drives the dramatic-structural teleology of Zemlinsky's work.

The first flashpoint occurs in bars 18–19 (Ex. 3). A disquieting moment of intensification and release, it also voices for the first time the chord which does

Ex. 3: *Maiblumen blühten überall,* harmonic models and voice-leading reduction

most to unsettle the tonal opening and to prohibit a large-scale, mixed-modal interpretation. To map Zemlinsky's tonal boundaries, this chord can be understood as a (half-)diminished minor seventh or, depending on its inversion and function, a minor added sixth. But more important here is that the chord is prolonged across the bar-line, as the harmonic model demonstrates. Already inverted within bar 18 to underscore its minor quality, the chord is transposed at the tritone and re-inverted in bar 19, ostensibly back to the local tonic (G-sharp minor). That Zemlinsky distributes the chord across over two octaves and adds the 'sixth' as the lowest voice prevents its recognition as a definitive diminished, minor or tonic chord. Rather, as both reductions show, the intervallic consistency of the harmonies and the coherence of their voice-leading bridge the dramatic shifts in articulation and rhythm. Their importance is such that, when they return in sequence three bars later, the 'dominant' sevenths with which they are paired pale beside their minor-diminished neighbours. Zemlinsky's harmonies are contrived – their recurrence proves so – but so too is his voice-leading, designed in this example to subvert harmonic norms.

Conversely, during the next textural episode from bar 38³, the chord is twice sandwiched between, and prolongs, G-flat major. More conventional, its function and distribution offer *Maiblumen*'s clearest example of how a registrally isolated motif in the upper voice bonds the usually distant triads beneath (tonic major, tritone minor). The surface-structural reaction to Zemlinsky's music is not unprecedented:

> Listening to a piece by Zemlinsky can be a kaleidoscopic experience, a series of shocks and involuntary memories which we may or may not choose to assemble into a coherent whole.[11]

Ex. 3: continued

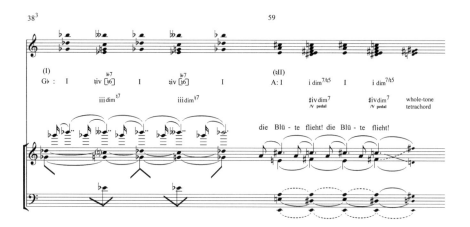

Indeed the climax of *Maiblumen* nearly a hundred bars later lends most support to a perspective which, on the largest scale, is associational rather than prolongational. Already an echo of bar 38³–41 in bars 59–60, now replete with a dominant pedal, had smudged the line between the minor added sixth chord and its diminished reading. But the authentic return of this amorphous chord (bar 133³⁻⁴) is Zemlinsky's vivid response to the death of the farm labourer, the object of the maid's affections. Entirely overshadowing an implied perfect cadence in F minor, this instrumental tutti passage also immediately follows the first occasion on which Zemlinsky rests all forces except the polarised duet of voice and second cello. Yet, creative difficulties appear to have halted Zemlinsky's progress soon after this dramatic pinnacle. To represent the maid's suicide in verse three with music 'more tragically serene' than that which accompanied the labourer's demise was perhaps too great a task as the composer's 'inspiration slacken[ed]'.[12] The theory squares with the suggestion that so reliant was Zemlinsky on 'the expressive, even hyper-expressive, nature of the sonorities that he tend[ed] to neglect other possibilities'.[13] If this comment, on the third of six Maeterlinck songs composed over a decade after *Maiblumen* ('Lied der Jungfrau', Op. 13, No. 3), encapsulates just how captivating Zemlinsky's Romantic sensibility could be, then it also alludes to the suspicion that his large-scale structures do not always convince.

Such misgivings trouble an 'ending' to *Maiblumen* that offers up further clues to the work's incompletion. The labourer's death triggers a 34-bar instrumental episode which is unusual in that ideas from both verses coincide. This reprise at first appears to endorse an interpretation of sonata form,[14] yet its introduction and conclusion suggest otherwise (Ex. 4). A quartet of violins and violas resumes the dramatic lead of the instruments through their terse, 'complaining' (*klagend*) response to death,

Ex. 3: continued

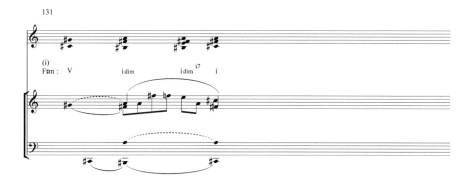

but its treble-dominated texture is a sign that, structurally, Zemlinsky's style remains fragmentary; his repeated rhythms mask material which is distantly related to the second verse but is now chromaticised in its gestures and voice-leading.[15] Silence defuses another climax at bar 160, before recollection of the second verse (violas and celli) relents to an imitative texture in which the first verse's original melody is shared across the final few bars. Zemlinsky did begin to set Dehmel's third verse; nonetheless it is notable that these first signs of conventional thematic reconciliation, however brief, led Zemlinsky down a creative and structural cul-de-sac.

* * *

'Zemlinsky can wait', read Schoenberg's backhanded compliment to his erstwhile mentor.[16] It is also a prophecy now much closer to being fulfilled. If it was too soon to speak of a 'Zemlinsky revival' in the mid nineties,[17] then the medley of events in the decade since has ensured that the reassessment of his achievements has been lasting.[18] *Maiblumen's* own revival is part of this, but its position within an accepted genre rests also upon the string sextet's conditions of performance. In this respect, historically the string sextet was ancillary to the string quartet: just as Franz Jellinek and Franz Schmidt joined the Rosé Quartet to perform *Verklärte Nacht,* two decades earlier two pupils of Joseph Joachim had augmented his quartet during their visit to England to perform Dvořák's String Sextet in A major, Op. 48; on their subsequent tour of the work they played it alongside his String Quartet in E-flat major, Op. 51. In the same country today, the young Aronowitz Ensemble serves the string sextet repertory though their complete line-up also features a piano. This enables performance of string and piano quintets, quartets and trios; indeed their versatility can be traced back to the violist whose name the ensemble honours. In 1950 Cecil

Ex. 4: *Maiblumen blühten überall*   bb. 137–141

Aronowitz co-founded the Melos Ensemble, a group whose aggregate fused a string quintet with a wind quintet and included a piano and harp, as the music required.[19] This elastic constitution, with programming to match, was a template for ensembles in their wake, particularly the London Sinfonietta and l'Ensemble Intercontemporain (founded 1968 and 1976 respectively).

So alive was Schoenberg to the possibilities of mixed ensembles that an attempted sequel to *Verklärte Nacht* – his own response to Dehmel's 'Ein Stelldichein' – was scored in 1905 for the unconventional ensemble of oboe, clarinet, piano, violin and cello. To suggest *Verklärte Nacht* may have stifled Schoenberg too, or that he suffered creative problems similar to those Zemlinsky faced in *Maiblumen*, would be unusual. Yet as its dimensions grew, *Ein Stelldichein* was abandoned.[20] Instead, then, it is overlooked as an ephemeral novelty caught equidistantly between the similarly configured 'Pierrot' ensemble and *Verklärte Nacht*. The mixed ensemble of 'Pierrot', especially, spawned a lineage so strong that it represents virtually all the major composers of the twentieth century. The mono-familial string sextet did not fare so well. Its symmetrical constitution, appealing visually, hampered efforts to maintain balance and inevitably promoted performance alongside, and comparisons with, the string quartet. But this did not concern Zemlinsky; the fuller textures of his string sextet articulate its dramatic structure but conceal its harmonic consistency: *Maiblumen* was not designed to be peripheral to a string quartet.

Ex. 4: continued

bb. 159–167 (end of published score)

Notes

1   Dahlhaus, C (1987) 'Schoenberg and programme music' ['Schönberg und die
    Programmusik', 1974], in *Schoenberg and the New Music*, trans. D Puffett and A Clayton,
    pp.94–104. Cambridge: Cambridge University Press, p.97.

2   For example, in his famous compendium of chamber music Walter Cobbett set the
    nonet as his upper limit; pragmatic, perhaps, but not the shrewdest response to the
    contemporaneous growth in 'ensemble' music and its vogue of doubling instruments.
    See Cobbett, WW (ed.) (1929–30) *Cobbett's Cyclopedic Survey of Chamber Music*, 2 vols.
    London: Oxford University Press, p.91.

3   Translations of the title vary: 'Maybuds blossomed all around' (Beaumont, A (2000)
    Zemlinsky. London: Faber. p.122), which preserves Dehmel's consonance, is perhaps
    superior to the literal though ambiguous 'May flowers bloom everywhere' (Gorrell, L
    (2002) *Discordant melody: Alexander Zemlinsky, his songs, and the Second Viennese
    school*. Westport: Greenwood Press, p.256 n12). Zemlinsky completed music for two of
    Dehmel's five stanzas.

4   The chromaticism (F flat-E double flat-D flat) in the first viola at this point derives from
    a harmonic scheme which alternates major and minor triads on G-flat: a typically
    Zemlinskyan gesture.

5   See Loll, W (1990) *Zwischen Tradition und Avantgarde: Die Kammermusik Alexander
    Zemlinskys*. Kassel: Bärenreiter, p.113. The related keys of the sextets – G-flat major
    (*Maiblumen*) and E-flat minor respectively – seem to have swayed his decision. As
    sketches for *Maiblumen* are undated, neither factor could be precise.

6   Weber, H (ed.) (1995), *Alexander Zemlinsky: Briefwechsel mit Arnold Schönberg, Alban
    Berg, Anton Webern und Franz Schreker*. Darmstadt: Wissenschaftliche Buchgesellschaft,
    p.12 (quoted by Beaumont, op. cit., p.122).
    „*Du musst unbedingt* die Sache noch einmal redigiren, herausgeben u. Verbreitung
    suchen." (Zemlinsky, letter to Schoenberg, 19 March 1902; emphasis his)
    Schoenberg would heed the advice, of course, and soon after describing his brother-in-
    law to Emil Hertzka as the 'best conductor alive' (Stein, E (ed.) (1964) *Arnold Schoenberg:
    Letters*, trans. E Wilkins and E Kaiser. London: Faber, p.46), Zemlinsky was the first to
    conduct the string-orchestral transcription of *Verklärte Nacht*.

7   Beaumont, 2006: private communication. See also Beaumont's chapter 'Zemlinsky
    Editions 1993–2007' in this book.

8   See Beaumont, 2000, p.123

9   Loll, op. cit., p.115

10 Beaumont, op. cit., p.122

11 Puffett, D (1996) 'Transcription and recomposition: the strange case of Zemlinsky's
    Maeterlinck songs', in *Analytical strategies and musical interpretation: Essays on
    nineteenth- and twentieth-century music*, C Ayrey and M Everist (eds), pp.72–119.
    Cambridge: Cambridge University Press, p.112.

12 Beaumont, op. cit., p.123

13 Puffett, op. cit., p.100

14 See Loll, op. cit., p.118–19

15 The relationship is retrograde-inversion, so it is revealed belatedly: compare the
    uppermost parts here (first violin, bars 140–1) with the start of verse two (first viola, bars
    104–5; Ex. 2). The rhythm does not change, but the bass-heavy instrumentation, a quartet
    of violas and cellos, is mirrored. Zemlinsky plays on the symmetry of the string sextet to
    delineate *Maiblumen*'s structure.

16 Schoenberg, A (1975) 'Zemlinsky' [1921] in *Style and Idea*, ed. L. Stein, pp.486–7. London:
    Faber, p.487.

17 Puffett, op. cit., p.73

18 The latest episode is the rediscovery of Zemlinsky's Cello Sonata, which prompted the
    conference (Middlesex University, 11 October 2006) from which these proceedings are
    taken. Before this, Zemlinsky scholarship had already grown, and coincided with the
    release of recordings and scores of most of his works.

19 Plans to form the ensemble were first hatched at a meeting between Aronowitz and the
    clarinettist Gervase de Peyer. Three further musicians, the flautist Richard Adeney,
    cellist Terence Weil and violinist Emanuel Hurwitz, were recruited as founder members.
    Together, they would 'step outside the normal repertory of trios and quartets' (Peyer, G de
    (1963) 'Problems of a Chamber Music Ensemble', *The Times* (14 January), p.12), although
    initially this agenda did not warrant the performance of much music from the twentieth
    century: Schubert's Octet, Beethoven's Septet and the Clarinet Quintets of Mozart and
    Brahms were the early mainstays of their repertoire.

20 Not one to repeat himself needlessly, Schoenberg probably realised *Ein Stelldichein*, with
    its distinctly Brahmsian harmonies, had begun to tread old ground.

Shoko Hino

Innovator or Imitator?
Examining Zemlinsky's Eclectic Voice in
Fantasies on Poems by Richard Dehmel, Op. 9

THEODOR ADORNO ONCE REMARKED that Zemlinsky's individuality was defined by his mixing of 'heterogeneous elements'.[1] This paradox, of being original through obvious borrowing, can be seen in his *Fantasies on Poems by Richard Dehmel*, Op. 9. As a fervent admirer of Brahms and Wagner, Zemlinsky immersed himself in their music and unreservedly incorporated their styles in this work. The structure is based on Brahms's technique of developing variation while his harmonic usage undoubtedly pays homage to Wagner's tonal language. But Zemlinsky's influences do not end with those frequently acknowledged composers. Bach's contrapuntal textures, the improvisatory atmosphere of Chopin's Nocturnes, and the poetic tradition of nineteenth-century lieder are strikingly notable in the *Dehmel Fantasies*. Given this list of influences, one might wonder what there is of Zemlinsky. This chapter answers that question by using the *Dehmel Fantasies* to search out and find Zemlinsky's voice within this cacophony of influences.

Zemlinsky's earlier piano works were written during his student days at the conservatory, and most exhibit the light, nonchalant qualities of salon music. He produced a total of fourteen solo piano compositions during his lifetime. A quick glance at their titles reveals two distinct categories: the absolute music aesthetic of the two Sonatas of 1887 and 1890; and the programmatic genres of the *Ländliche Tänze* Op. 1 of 1892. However, only in the *Fantasies* do we see the emergence of Zemlinsky's individual voice, revealing the sophisticated artistic sensibility of the 27-year-old composer. Unlike the firework pieces of composers who wrote only for the sake of virtuosity, the piano writing in Zemlinsky's *Fantasies* is simple, elegant, charming and undeniably lyrical, despite the 'incredible technique' he possessed as a pianist.[2]

Composed in 1898, *Fantasies on Poems by Richard Dehmel*, Op. 9 is Zemlinsky's last substantial work for piano. The years which immediately precede and follow this work saw the completion of the operas *Sarema* (1896), *Es war einmal* (1897–9), the Symphony in B-flat major (1897), and a considerable number of lieder. It is unclear whether or not a public performance took place. What we do know is that immediately after its publication in 1901, he wrote to his former student, Alma Schindler: 'I'd like to dedicate the volume to you, I must do so. But your name should not appear, that would be compromising. What should I do? Think it over!'[3] This cryptic note can be explained by a crisis in Zemlinsky's relationship with the soprano Melanie Guttmann, with whom he collaborated frequently in performances, during the composition of the *Fantasies*. She had decided that her future lay in America, to where she eventually emigrated and got married. Antony Beaumont speculates on a connection of this painful circumstance in Zemlinsky's life to a line of Dehmel's poem in the third *Fantasie*, originally entitled 'Ideale Landschaft' (*Ideal Countryside*): 'Und sahst nur immer weg von mir, Ins Licht, ins Licht' (*You turned your gaze away from me, towards the light*) which reflected Melanie's eyes looking towards a new life in America.[4] After the work's completion, Zemlinsky felt this particular poem showed his personal crisis too obviously. He solved this rather sensitive issue by substituting Dehmel's poem, 'Liebe' (*Love*) for the original one.

Zemlinsky's only attempt to set music to Dehmel's poetry is found in the Op. 7 lieder of 1899 and *Fünf Lieder* from 1907. However, the *Fantasies* were Zemlinsky's first engagement with this controversial poet. The two had never met, but like the progressive composers of this period, Zemlinsky was strongly drawn to Dehmel's fearless and charismatic expression. Wilhelm Kahle wrote, 'The young generation of today cannot imagine the enthusiasm with which the youth at the turn of the century exalted the poetry and personality of Dehmel.'[5] Throughout his career, Dehmel explored and openly spoke of his beliefs about love and sex, as well as his individual socio-political perspectives. The earliest musical settings of Dehmel's poetry were the 1895 lieder of Conrad Ansorge. Strauss used Dehmel's poetry in some of his early lieder. Zemlinsky's student Schoenberg wrote to the poet 'Your poems have had a decisive influence on my development as a composer'[6] and wrote the string sextet *Verklärte Nacht* in the same year, 1898, as the *Fantasies*.

Upon hearing the *Fantasies*, one first notices their simplicity. The rhythms are basic, texture is generally thin and light, voice-leading is conventional, and the form is strophic ABA' with a coda derived from the A material. All movements are short, the longest being under four minutes. Each movement's brevity reflects not only the characteristic focus of lieder, but also the compositional aesthetic of the Second Viennese School, characterised by concentration of expression.

In the first *Fantasie*, 'Stimme des Abends' (*Voice of the Night*) Zemlinsky captures the quiet atmosphere of the night by using a dynamic range progressing from *pianissimo* in the first bar to *pianississimo* in the seventh, ending *pianissississimo* in bar 30 (see Ex. 1):

Ex. 1

bb. 1–3:

bb. 19–21:

bb. 30–33:

This extreme soft range is a feature also commonly found in many of Zemlinsky's lieder. Along with this delicate dynamic level, the mysterious mood of the night is represented by tonal ambiguity. The key signature is E-flat major, but Zemlinsky begins the opening theme on F-sharp, the enharmonic third of E-flat minor, which immediately moves to G, the major third of the stated key. After this E-flat minor and major oscillation, we hear the pristine sonority of E-flat major in the third bar. The gentle dynamic level coupled with the juxtaposition of E-flat minor and major not only enhances the hazy sound-world of the night, but also reflects the aesthetic of Art Nouveau-based *Jugendstil*, in which artists, including composers, often explored ambiguity to suggest rather than to define their ideas.

This half-step movement – the upward resolution of the appoggiatura – serves another important purpose: the organisational kernel of developing variation structure, a truly Brahmsian compositional principle. Zemlinsky's choice of 'developing variation' undoubtedly reflects a general trend in this period: 'among my colleagues it was considered praiseworthy to compose in as "Brahmsian" a manner as possible'.[7]

The improvisatory style created by a lyrical melody over an arpeggiated and chordal accompaniment is a feature of the Nocturnes for piano by Field and Chopin and, like theirs, Zemlinsky's lyricism is attributed to his love of opera and singing. Beaumont noted that 'as the story goes, Zemlinsky would sometimes break into a song, or rather a wordless caterwaul of moans and groans.'[8] But in contrast to his forerunners' use of elaborate melodic ornamentation to emulate the bel-canto style of singing, Zemlinsky retains the original melody note by note in its return, free from any embellishment. For example, in the second *Fantasie* entitled 'Waldseligkeit' (*Forest Joy*), the return of the A section melody is exactly the same as the opening. But by adding a new accompanimental layer of semiquavers in its return, Zemlinsky enhances the 'murmuring' sound of the forest as stated in the poem and reduces the dynamic level to *pianississimo*. This particular compositional device of preserving the original melody and modifying what surrounds it is frequently evident in Zemlinsky's works.

Ex. 2

bb. 1–3

bb. 16–19

bb. 52–56

This improvisatory atmosphere is created by the interpolation of 'sighs' between the lyrical melodies, the brief passages of harmonic movement that connect the phrases. In the first movement, this is clearly heard in the swift fluttering figure which links the ends and beginnings of the contrapuntal themes, remarkably reminiscent of Bach's polyphonic writing, the slowly moving theme presented in stretto, appearing first in the tenor, followed by the alto and soprano voices, each entering half a bar later.

Ex. 3

bb.1–5

In the second *Fantasie,* the subordinate quaver arpeggio accompaniment beneath the melody in the opening two bars emerges as a lyrical duet in thirds while the melody exhales on a dotted minim.

Ex. 4

bb. 1–3

This duet depicts the first line of the poem, 'The forest begins to murmur', vividly recalling Wagner's forest scenery.

Schumann's characteristic use of the mediant key relationship, as in many of his lieder, is found in the second *Fantasie,* and is dictated by the poem's structure; the first stanza (F-sharp major) speaks of the gentle movement of the trees, and the second stanza (D major) of a man's solitude (shown in Ex. 2).

In the third *Fantasie,* 'Liebe' (*Love*), we hear a love duet between the right and left hand, back and forth. This aria-like melody lasts for twelve bars, the entirety of the A section. A sudden shift from D major to D minor not only resembles Schubert's characteristic modal shifts but also Zemlinsky's own belief in key symbolism.

Ex. 5

bb. 1–4:

For Zemlinsky, D major signified reconciliation, whereas D minor meant tragic despair. This abrupt shift from major to minor fills even the warm tone of D Major with Zemlinsky's intense pessimism, his suppressed sadness and longing – 'My cry of pain re-echoed in the distance', as expressed in the poem.

In this movement we also find a kaleidoscope of chromatic harmonies, reminiscent of Wagner's harmonic language. Starting from the anacrusis to bar 21, an outburst of rich chromatic harmonies pours out, over a span of four bars before the return of the A' section.

Ex. 6

bb. 19–22:

Zemlinsky exhausts the potential of the half-step movement, a device which permits the music to travel even to the remotest key. But there is more: Zemlinsky groups these expanded chords into three groups of four semiquavers, each group entering on the weak beat. This completely demolishes the metric regularity temporarily, creating a hemiola effect as the emotions run high in this climactic passage.

The last *Fantasie*, 'Käferlied' (*Maybug*), is the shortest, lasting just under two minutes. Also called 'common cockchafer', 'May bug', 'Maybug', or 'May beetle', it is a large European beetle that is destructive to foliage, flowers, and fruit as an adult and to plant roots as a larva. In the British Isles, the name 'cockchafer' refers more broadly to any of the beetles in the subfamily Melolonthinae (family Scarabaeidae), which are known in North America as 'June beetles', 'June bugs', or 'May beetles'.[9]

Though somewhat rarely represented in music the importance of this Maybug should not be underestimated; the burgeoning spring language of insects, flowers and tree was frequently used by *Jugendstil* artists to symbolise hidden yearnings, especially eroticism, at which Dehmel hints through the Maybug. The fourth *Fantasie* is absolutely charming in character. Zemlinsky entertains us with the humorous musical imitation of the Maybug's buzzing by employing trills and written-out trills.

Ex. 7

bb. 1–4

bb. 62–65

The left hand provides a syncopated ländler accompaniment throughout, juxtaposing the refined and the banal – a characteristic of Mahler. Equally associated with Mahler is 'progressive' tonality. The key signature is A major, but the work begins in D major, briefly touches F-sharp minor in the third bar but returns to D major, shortly moving to A major, for only two bars. We hear a definite, clear cadence in D major in bar 23, though it ends firmly in F-sharp major.

Unlike Chopin who often gave detailed pedal indications, Zemlinsky seems relatively unconcerned with pedalling. The absence of pedal markings in the *Fantasies* may be attributed to an impatience caused by Zemlinsky's rigorous schedule as a performing pianist. Schoenberg remembers Zemlinsky as a *Schnellschreiber* (speed-writer): 'While waiting for the ink to dry on a page of manuscript he would practice for the next concert.'[10] In spite of this lack of precision in pedalling, he endowed each movement with a very specific character marking: *Sehr ruhig und durchaus leise* ('Very quiet and soft throughout'), *Ungemein zart und leicht bewegt* ('Deeply tender and lightly moving'), *Sehr langsam und innig* ('Very slow and heartfelt'), *Grazios leicht bewegt* ('Graceful, light with motion'). These directions, combined with the individual poems, provide each *Fantasie* with a unique sound world, similar to the distinct atmosphere of an opera scene. His passion for opera, as well as his love of intimate expression of lieder, is to be found in the *Dehmel Fantasies*.

Tracing through the *Fantasies*, we find Zemlinsky perhaps trying to ease the polemic tension of the musical scene in the late 19th century between the traditionalist view of Brahms, supported by Hanslick, who promoted the purity of absolute instrumental music, as opposed to the New German School formerly led by Liszt and Wagner, who advocated the extra-musical associations of programmatic music. What makes the *Fantasies* distinct from Zemlinsky's own earlier piano compositions as well as the vast ocean of solo piano repertoire by other composers is the fusion of the solo piano genre with poetry. Although the blending of artistic and literary expression emerged during the 19th century and was central to the Romantic aesthetic, it is rare to find an entire work based so specifically on poetry. Schumann's *Fantasie* Op. 17 is based on a philosophical quotation from Friedrich Schlegel, and the first movement of Brahms's *Ballade* Op. 10 was inspired by a Scottish poem 'Edward' by Johann Gottfried Herder, but both of these have sections unrelated to the poetry. Even Liszt's three *Sonnets de Petrarch* from *Années de Pèlerinage* Book II were first conceived as lieder for tenor and piano, only later being transcribed for solo piano.

Zemlinsky's innovatory *Fantasies* might be best understood as 'Songs without Words', in which words are inadequate or too daring to express strong personal emotions. Thus, the intense longing of both Dehmel and Zemlinsky is present, as in the New German School, but 'hidden between the notes', reflecting Brahms's traditional attitude.

Unlike Schubert who, in his lieder, tended to keep voice and piano separate, Schumann was the first to attempt to integrate the two. Zemlinsky furthered this process by creating a new genre. By transforming the lied into a work for solo piano, Zemlinsky caused the invisible wall between the accompanist and the singer to vanish, assigning to the pianist exclusive responsibility and authority.

This innovation consequently poses a new and unique challenge for the pianist who chooses to perform the *Fantasies*. While not technically difficult, Zemlinsky's

Fantasies require mature and sensitive interpretation. We do not know what inspired Zemlinsky to venture into the *Dehmel Fantasies*, but its unique conception may be attributed to his ability as an exceptional collaborator. One source tells us, 'When Zemlinsky sits at the piano, accompanying cannot be discussed in a conventional sense. He is not an accompanist but a master of the composer. He takes command and illuminates the work. When he performs *Winterreise...* the smallest interlude receives unsuspected significance...'.[11]

The existence of the *Fantasies* is scarcely known, as he did not write much for the piano and he is largely known as an opera composer. Therefore, it is pleasant to learn of an arrangement for clarinet and piano by James Breed, published by Doblinger in 1989. The only difference between the arrangement and the original is that the melodic material is given to the clarinet part, while the piano plays everything else. While the original *Fantasies* have been recorded by three pianists, Siegfried Mauser (1995), Marco Rapetti (2002), and Silke Avenhaus (2005), the clarinet arrangement has not yet been recorded.

Where, in all these various influences, can we find Zemlinsky's voice? It may be clearly heard in his successful integration of the musical languages of diverse composers. Adorno remarked that 'Zemlinsky's claim to authority, which his Viennese friends always acknowledged, was based on the balancing of these disparate energies in his work in a most productive way.'[12] The *Dehmel Fantasies* illuminates Zemlinsky as a versatile musician, a master of small-scale lieder as well as of large-scale opera. Zemlinsky's internalisation of Dehmel's poems gave birth to a work with imagery and a sound world of its own, in an emerging new genre, through which we can perceive Zemlinsky's rare and eclectic voice.

Notes

1   Adorno, Theodor W (1963) *Quasi una Fantasia. Musikalische Schriften II.* Frankfurt, p.160.

2   Hailey, Christopher (1993) *Franz Schreker, 1878–1934: A Cultural Biography.* Cambridge: Cambridge University Press, p.2.

3   Beaumont, Antony (2000) *Zemlinsky.* Ithaca: Cornell University Press, also London: Faber and Faber p.47.

4   Ibid.

5   Kahle, Wilhelm (1954) *Geschichte der deutschen Dichtun.* Münster, Germany, p.338.

6   Schoenberg, Arnold (1965) *Arnold Schoenberg Letters.* Trans. Eithne Wilkens and Ernst Kaiser. Selected and ed. Erwin Stein. New York, p.35.

7   Alexander Zemlinsky (1922) 'Brahms und die neuere Generation: persönliche Erinnerungen', *Musikblätter des Anbruch* 4, pp.69–70.

8   Beaumont, op. cit., p.xv

9   *Encyclopædia Britannica* (2007) 'Cockchafer', *Encyclopædia Britannica Online*. 29 pr. 2007 http://www.search.eb.com/eb/article-9024583

10 Schoenberg, Arnold (1972) *Style and Idea*. Trans. Leo Black. Ed. Leonard Stein. New York, p.55.

11 Quoted in Tancsik, Pamela (2000) 'Die Prager Oper heist Zemlinsky,' *Theatergeschichte des Neuen Deutschen Theaters Prag in der Ära Zemlinsky von 1911 bis 1927*. Vienna: Böhlau Verlag, p.515.

12 Adorno, op. cit., p. 357

Steven Vande Moortele

Form as Context: Zemlinsky's Second String Quartet and the Tradition of Two-Dimensional Sonata Form

Contexts and canonicity

SINCE THE LATE 1980s musicology has witnessed a distinct shift from monologic to dialogic readings of musical compositions.[1] Rather than continuing the study of self-contained 'works' and emphasising each individual composition's originality, recent scholarship has tended to relate individual compositions explicitly to other compositions or to a larger corpus of works, and to comment especially on the links that exist between several compositions. This tendency becomes apparent not only in several overt transfers of the concept of intertextuality to the field of music such as those by, among others, Kevin Korsyn[2] and Michael Klein[3]. The dialogic is also central to James Hepokoski and Warren Darcy's much more mainstream and very influential 'Sonata Theory', in which a specific composition is seen as entertaining a sophisticated dialogue with the complex constellation of available options that constitutes the idea of sonata form.[4]

Common to all these approaches is that they attempt to analyse 'in context' (context for the purposes of this chapter being defined narrowly as a collection of musical texts) an 'ecology'[5] in which several compositions coexist. Needless to say, a composition always figures in a multitude of contexts, and equally obvious is the fact that the choice of a context within which to discuss a certain composition is not neutral. Meaning, importance and, ultimately, canonic status of a composition are at least partly dependent on its contexts, the position it occupies within these contexts and the degree to which one or several of these contexts lend themselves to the development of a broader discourse.

Canon formation is a much more complex phenomenon than this, of course; yet reflecting on the role of contexts in this process might offer opportunities for Zemlinsky scholarship.[6] For canonicity and Zemlinsky, it seems, are two things that don't go well together. Not even the staunchest defender of Zemlinsky's music would claim that any one of his compositions has managed to acquire canonic status, even if that canonicity is limited to the kind that ensures a piece of its place in the academy rather than in the concert hall. At the very best, a number of Zemlinsky's pieces continue to hibernate on the verges of the canon: the *Sechs Gesänge*, Op. 13, *Eine florentinische Tragödie*, Op. 16, the *Lyrische Symphonie*, Op. 18, and, maybe most of all – especially as far as the scholarly canon is concerned – the Second String Quartet, Op. 15.

The Second String Quartet has been granted pride of place in several of the most important contributions to Zemlinsky scholarship.[7] These discussions have, however, taken place mainly in contexts that remain uninterested in connecting to a broader musicological discourse. As a result, the Quartet's impact outside specialised Zemlinsky studies has largely been restricted to the odd footnote in literature on other works by other composers. In this chapter, I will try to frame Zemlinsky's *Second String Quartet* in a new context and demonstrate how that might offer opportunities to get this piece involved in a discourse that transcends traditional Zemlinsky studies and thus more likely to influence canon formation.

Contexts for Zemlinsky

When thinking of Zemlinsky's Second String Quartet, written between 1913 and 1915 when its composer was music director of the Neues Deutsches Theater in Prague, several contexts that might be useful for its interpretation immediately spring to mind. Some of the most obvious include the personal context of Zemlinsky's oeuvre – or part thereof, for instance the works from his Prague years; the generic context of the string quartet or, again, part thereof; and the regional/contemporary contexts of music, chamber music or string quartets written in Prague during the first decades of the twentieth century. The first of these contexts, Zemlinsky's oeuvre, is the one within which the Second String Quartet has most frequently been discussed in Zemlinsky studies – naturally. The context of contemporary music in Prague in the early twentieth century, by contrast, seems to have been somewhat overlooked and merits closer inspection. Particularly enlightening might be a detailed comparison with the 1911 Second String Quartet, Op. 31 by the Prague composer Josef Suk – Dvořák's son-in-law – which is, like Zemlinsky's Second, in one movement.

In this chapter I will discuss two other contexts, which are made up by two interrelated groups of works that share a number of peculiar musical aspects – mainly regarding formal organisation – with Zemlinsky's Second String Quartet: Arnold Schoenberg's instrumental compositions from the beginning of the twentieth century, and the tradition of what I call two-dimensional sonata form in Germanic art music since Franz Liszt. There are several reasons why it seems obvious to consider Zemlinsky's Second String Quartet in the context of Schoenberg's early instrumental music. The earliest reference to the Second String Quartet can be found in a letter to

Schoenberg from 20 July 1913, in which Zemlinsky informed his friend and brother-in-law that he was 'working steadily on a – string quartet!!'[8] On a postcard a few days later Zemlinsky revealed that this string quartet was to be in 'only one movement, that is to say four parts in one movement' and was 'apparently in F-sharp minor'.[9] Almost one and a half years later, on New Year's Eve 1914, he announced that he intended to dedicate it to Schoenberg.[10] The combination of its formal organisation, its key and its dedicatee strongly suggests that Zemlinsky's Second String Quartet is closely related to some of the instrumental music Schoenberg had composed in the years before. It shares its key with Schoenberg's Second String Quartet Op.10, while its formal organisation is similar to that of Schoenberg's First String Quartet Op. 7, his First Chamber Symphony Op. 9 and the symphonic poem *Pelleas und Melisande* Op. 5.

This evident and oft-invoked context is, however, nested in a larger context. For Schoenberg's large-scale instrumental compositions from the years between 1902 and 1906 themselves prominently figure in the much broader and older tradition of two-dimensional sonata form: the combination of the movements of a sonata cycle and the sections of a sonata form at the same hierarchical level of a single-movement composition. A two-dimensional sonata form consists basically of an overarching sonata form in which the movements of a (multi-movement) sonata cycle are interpolated between or coincide with units of the sonata form. Both dimensions of the form – that of the overarching sonata form and that of the sonata cycle – span the entire composition; only by referring to both of them can the formal course of the piece be explained in a satisfactory way. Probably inspired by models from the first half of the nineteenth century – particularly the finale of Beethoven's Ninth Symphony and Schubert's *Wanderer* Fantasy – this pattern of formal organisation came to flourish in several of Liszt's single-movement instrumental works from his Weimar period and was later adopted most notably by Richard Strauss in a number of his tone poems. It was most probably through Strauss that at the beginning of the twentieth century, two-dimensional sonata form found its way to the young Schoenberg.[11]

Central to a dialogic approach to Zemlinsky's Second String Quartet is that in any of the aforementioned contexts, it takes on both an active and a passive role. Not only is our interpretation of Zemlinsky's Second String Quartet coloured by its position vis-à-vis the other pieces in the context; it can also be seen as engaging in a dialogue – intentional or not – with these other pieces, adopting some of their characteristics, rejecting others, and maybe sometimes finding new solutions for similar problems. For us to be able to properly assess the historical position and the aesthetic value of Zemlinsky's Second String Quartet, it is necessary that we investigate whether the piece engages in a dialogue only with Schoenberg's instrumental compositions from the previous decade, or enters into a dialogue with the problems and the conventions of the tradition of two-dimensional sonata form as such – a tradition in which Schoenberg's contributions evidently play a role as well. If the context for Zemlinsky's Quartet is limited to Schoenberg's early instrumental music, the latter's overwhelming historical importance tends to overshadow it. In this context, it risks being regarded merely as a belated appendix to Schoenberg's output; the nine years that separate its completion from that of Schoenberg's final two-dimensional sonata form, the Chamber Symphony Op. 9, are a very long time measured against the speed with which new music was evolving in Schoenberg's hands at the time.[12] If, by contrast, it can be shown that Zemlinsky's Second String Quartet is an autonomous agent in the broader tradition of two-dimensional sonata form since the middle of the nineteenth century, this might offer opportunities to discuss it with a fresh and more open frame of mind.

Form in the Second String Quartet

In the next few paragraphs I will investigate the form of Zemlinsky's Second String Quartet by way of a comparison with Schoenberg's First String Quartet and First Chamber Symphony as well as, more implicitly, with the concept of two-dimensional sonata form as such. This will reveal a number of striking similarities to Schoenberg's two-dimensional sonata forms, but also a number of significant differences. It will also reveal that at one crucial instance, Zemlinsky deploys a formal strategy that cannot be found in any of Schoenberg's two-dimensional sonata forms.[13]

Zemlinsky's Second String Quartet versus Schoenberg's First String Quartet

Because of the analogies in both genre and formal organisation, it is an obvious choice to compare Zemlinsky's Second String Quartet with Schoenberg's First String Quartet. In both two-dimensional sonata forms, the basic relationship of the movements of the sonata cycle to the overarching sonata form is identical: the first movement of the sonata cycle coincides with units of the overarching sonata form, while all three subsequent movements are interpolated between units of the overarching form. This similarity seems all the more striking given that, as far as I can see, these are the only two-dimensional sonata forms in which all movements but the first are interpolated.

Still, the overall formal plan of both compositions is similar only in the most general of ways. As will become clear later in this chapter, the identification of the first movement with units of the overarching sonata form is realised in a very different way in both compositions. The position of the interpolated movements in the overarching sonata form is different as well, as is shown in Fig. 1.

In Schoenberg's First String Quartet, the scherzo is interpolated in the middle of the development, the slow movement in the middle of the recapitulation and the finale between the recapitulation and the coda of the overarching sonata form.

In Zemlinsky's Second String Quartet, the finale is interpolated between the recapitulation and the coda as well. The slow movement and the scherzo, however, appearing here in inverse order, are treated as one large interpolated block that is inserted between the short development and the recapitulation.

Schoenberg, First String Quartet			Zemlinsky, Second String Quartet		
Bars	Form	Cycle	Bars	Form	Cycle
1–199	Exposition	First movement	1–179	Exposition	First movement
200–398	Development 1		180–263	Development	
399–783	------------	Scherzo	264–360	------------	Slow movement
784–908	Development 2	------------	361–744	------------	Scherzo
909–951	Recapitulation 1		755–823	Recapitulation	------------
952–1067	------------	Slow movement			
1068–1121	Recapitulation 2	------------			
1122–1269	------------	Finale	824–1136	------------	Finale
1270–1320	Coda		1137–1221	Coda	------------

Fig. 1: Formal overviews of Schoenberg's First and Zemlinsky's Second String Quartet

An additional difference between the interpolated movements in Schoenberg's First String Quartet and Zemlinsky's Second String Quartet is that in the Schoenberg Quartet the interpolated movements are more strongly integrated into the overarching sonata form. To be sure, the beginning of the scherzo is singled out by a shocking modulation from F major to G-flat major. During its final large formal unit (bars 706ff), however, this interpolated movement gradually acquires a developmental texture announcing the return of the development of the overarching sonata form from bar 735 onwards. The functionalisation of the subsequent movements is more unambiguous. The slow movement is closely associated thematically with the second part of the recapitulation that follows it, and in terms of key relationships, both the slow movement and the finale (in A minor and major respectively) function as a large-scale dominant preparation for the definitive D major tonic arrival at the beginning of the coda. In Zemlinsky's Second String Quartet, no traces of a similar far-reaching functionalisation of the interpolated movements in the formal course of the overarching sonata form can be found.

Zemlinsky's Second String Quartet versus Schoenberg's First Chamber Symphony

The most salient feature Zemlinsky's Second String Quartet has in common with Schoenberg's First Chamber Symphony is the use of a motto. Yet the nature of these mottoes is very different in both compositions. In Schoenberg's Chamber Symphony, the motto is clearly defined (Ex. 1).

Ex. 1: Different shapes of the motto in Schoenberg's First Chamber Symphony

Although it sometimes occurs in shapes that evidently differ from its original shape – it can be verticalised, inverted or stripped of its rhythmical pregnancy – none of these shapes contributes to even a small-scale variational or developmental process, and none of them affects the diastematic content of the motto. Whatever form it assumes, the motto always remains directly linked to its original shape. As a result, its identity as a motto is always apparent.

This is not always the case in Zemlinsky's Quartet. Here, the motto is presented in the form of a sentence (Ex. 2).

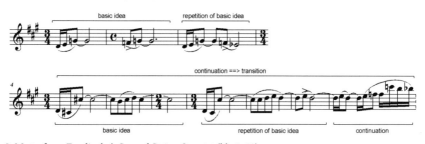

Ex. 2: Motto from Zemlinsky's Second String Quartet (bb. 1–10)

Bars 1–2 present a basic idea, bar 3 brings its compressed repetition, and bars 4–10 constitute a continuation that merges into a transition to the main theme that enters in bar 11. Interestingly, the continuation itself is structured as a sentence as well, with bars 4–5 as a basic idea, bars 6–7 as the repetition of the basic idea, and bars 8–10 as the continuation.[14] As a result, the motto is not only much longer in comparison to that in Schoenberg's Chamber Symphony, it also gains a thematic quality, which yields a thematic treatment of the motto in the further course of the composition. If one insists on distinguishing a concisely formulated motto, a possibility might be to consider bars 1–3 as the actual motto and bars 1–10 as a whole as a motto group or motto theme. In this case, however, one must realise that when the motto returns in the further course of the composition – as often as not under the guise of a new variant – bars 4–10 can be repeated or varied independently, i.e. without a preceding statement of bars 1–3, thus functioning as a substitute for the actual motto.

In spite of these differences, the motto largely serves the same purposes in both compositions. A number of these functions are identical to those which mottoes traditionally serve in nineteenth- and early twentieth-century symphonic and chamber music. A motto can operate as a unifying factor, because of its frequent recurrences over the entire course or in all movements of a composition, or because the thematic material of the different movements is derived from it. For the same reasons – and also simply because it is placed at the beginning of the composition – it can exert a decisive influence on a composition's identity. Finally, it can help to articulate the form, by returning at major formal junctions throughout the composition.

All of these traditional functions can be observed in both Schoenberg's First Chamber Symphony and Zemlinsky's Second String Quartet. In either piece, the motto very clearly plays a role in determining the work's identity as well as in the unification of its different formal units. In Schoenberg's Chamber Symphony, the motto is first played near the beginning of the composition and although none of the other themes is derived from it, it is present at important formal junctures throughout the composition.

In Zemlinsky's Quartet too, the motto is presented at the very beginning of the composition. Here as well, the motto – or its substitute – returns numerous times in the further course of the composition. Additionally, and in contrast to Schoenberg's Chamber Symphony, the main themes of both the interpolated slow movement and the scherzo are clearly derived from the motto (Ex. 3).

Ex. 3: Derivation of themes from the motto

In addition to these traditional functions, the mottoes in both compositions fulfil a number of functions that are exclusively related to the concept of two-dimensional sonata form. Most obviously, the form-articulating function of the motto can serve to mark a so-called dimensional shift: the transition from one dimension to another that takes place at those spots where the relationship between the different dimensions changes. Especially in Schoenberg's Chamber Symphony, the motto almost systematically appears near the borders of those movements from the sonata cycle that are interpolated in the overarching sonata form. In Zemlinsky's String Quartet, dimensional shifts are somewhat less clearly profiled. The motto resounds in bars 254–263, 745–756 and 1137–1145, i.e. before the slow movement, after the scherzo and after the finale. Since there is no dimensional shift between the slow movement and the scherzo, it is only at the beginning of the finale that the motto is actually 'missing'. Yet in contrast to Schoenberg's Chamber Symphony, where the form-articulating capacity of the motto on the largest scale is increased by its limited presence within the formal units of the overarching sonata form, the motto in Zemlinsky's Quartet has an important role to play within the dimensions of the form. This considerably limits its potential to articulate the dimensional shifts. As a result, and in contrast to Schoenberg's Chamber Symphony, the motto in Zemlinsky's Quartet does not primarily articulate the interpolated movements, but is mainly involved in the identification of the exposition of the overarching sonata form with the first movement of the sonata cycle.

Beyond the Schoenberg context

When a movement of the sonata cycle is identified with units of the overarching sonata form, they coincide in such a way that characteristic elements of both dimensions are combined into one formal unit, which thus is capable of functioning simultaneously as part of the overarching sonata form and as a movement in the sonata cycle. This identification is one of the thorniest issues a composer of a two-dimensional sonata form has to confront. He must find a way to reconcile the non-identical, sometimes even opposing functions of the different dimensions that have to be fulfilled simultaneously by the same formal unit.

For the identification of the first movement of the sonata cycle with units of the overarching sonata form, Zemlinsky has found a very ingenious solution, realising a well-nigh perfect match of that first movement onto the overarching sonata form's exposition. It is not very difficult to distinguish the outlines of a sonata form exposition in Zemlinsky's Quartet. The motto theme is followed by a main theme group in bars 11–49, a transition in bars 50–122, a subsidiary theme group in bars 123–160 and a closing group in bars 161–179. Upon closer scrutiny, a number of features of this exposition might strike one as somewhat unusual. The main theme group, for instance, has a rather complex organisation. It consists of a binary theme (bars 11–15 and 16–18) that is separated from a transformation of its second part (bars 25–39) by a varied and extended return of the motto (bars 19–24). Another passage that is derived from the motto (bars 40–49) links the main theme group to the next large formal unit. Between the standing on the dominant at the end of the transition and the beginning of the subsidiary theme group, a third varied return of the motto group is inserted. Finally and most importantly, the tonal relationship between main and subsidiary theme groups is unusual. It is most striking that the subsidiary theme group basically is in D major. The main theme group having started in D minor, this is, of course, a rather unusual key for a subsidiary theme group. One could argue that the beginning of the exposition is not in D minor, but – given the key signature – in F-sharp minor. Yet F-sharp is a shadow tonic at most – remember Zemlinsky writing to Schoenberg that his quartet was only 'apparently in F-sharp minor'. At the very beginning of the piece, the suggested key is G minor, and although there is an unmistakable F-sharp minor triad in bar 4, the main theme group clearly takes off in D minor (flavoured by an added augmented fourth). To be sure, the rest of the main theme's harmonic organisation is anything but straightforward, but nothing indicates that it should be heard in F-sharp rather than in D minor.

One cannot expect a sonata form written around 1910 by a first-rate composer like Zemlinsky to be an obedient reproduction of the models offered in many nineteenth-century textbooks. Still, it would be desirable not only to marvel at Zemlinsky's originality, but also to find some kind of explanation as to why exactly he designed his exposition the way he did. In this particular case, the reason why Zemlinsky's exposition is organised in such a peculiar way is that its segments simultaneously have to function as the sections of an entire sonata form. Only the motto fulfils the same function in both dimensions. All subsequent units have a double function: the main theme group of the exposition in the overarching sonata form is a complete exposition in the first movement of the sonata cycle, the transition a development, the subsidiary theme group a recapitulation and the closing group a coda (see Fig. 2).

The simultaneous function of what is the main theme group in one dimension and a complete exposition in the other explains its complex organisation. From the point of view of the dimension of the cycle – the first movement of the multi-movement design – bars 11–18 can be regarded as a main theme, bars 19–24 as a transition and bars 25–40 as a subsidiary theme. The tonal relationship between bars 105–160 and bars 11–49 too becomes less strange if it is not exclusively regarded as that between a main and a subsidiary theme, but as one between a recapitulation and an exposition as well. The overall harmonic organisation of bars 1–179 is indeed that of a sonata form rather than that of a sonata form's exposition. The double function equally explains the presence of a return of the motto between the transition – whose pronounced developmental character probably is no coincidence either – and the beginning of the subsidiary theme. Although it constitutes a tonal

return, the subsidiary theme itself cannot possibly be regarded as a thematic return
of the formal unit starting in bar 11. Rather, it genuinely incorporates the thematic
contrast it is expected to have in an exposition. A sense of thematic return is effected
by the reprise of the motto, bars 105–109 being quasi identical to bars 3–4. Given
the requirements of the dimension of the form, the thematic return necessary to
the dimension of the cycle could not possibly have been realised as a return of
the main theme in the formal unit that functions as the overarching sonata form's
subsidiary theme. Instead, it has been substituted by a recapitulation of the formal
unit immediately preceding its main theme in the formal unit immediately before
its subsidiary theme.

Bars	Overarching sonata form	First movement
1–10	Exposition Motto theme	Exposition Motto theme
11–18	Main theme group First part	Main theme
19–24	Motto theme	Motto theme
25–39	Second part (transformation)	Subsidiary theme
40–49	Transition	Transition
50–104	Transition	Development
105–122	Motto theme	Recapitulation
123–160	Subsidiary theme	
161–179	Closing group	Coda

Fig. 2: Identification of exposition and first movement in Zemlinsky's Second String Quartet

By identifying the first movement of the sonata cycle with the exposition of the
overarching sonata form in this specific way, Zemlinsky expands the context for
the interpretation of his quartet beyond the realm of Schoenberg's large-scale tonal
instrumental works. The strategy Zemlinsky deploys does not occur in any of his
brother-in-law's two-dimensional sonata forms. Schoenberg's standard solution for
this kind of problem is to identify the first movement of the cycle with the exposition
and part of the development of the form. In the First String Quartet, for example, only
the exposition of first movement of the sonata cycle coincides with the exposition
of the overarching form, the latter's development containing a varied repeat of the
exposition that functions as the recapitulation in the dimension of the cycle.

The composition that is closest to Zemlinsky's String Quartet in this respect is much older. It is Liszt's Piano Sonata in B minor from 1853, to many the *locus classicus* of two-dimensional sonata form. Here as well, the local sonata form is identified with the exposition of the overarching sonata form, the former's exposition coinciding with the latter's main theme group, the development with the transition and the recapitulation with the subsidiary theme group. Zemlinsky adopts Liszt's strategy, but does not blindly copy it. Rather, he intensifies and indeed refines it by modifying the tonal relationship between main and subsidiary theme groups as well as by his use of the motto.

Form as context

It will have become clear from the above not only that Zemlinsky's Second String Quartet is more than a mere copy of the two-dimensional sonata forms Schoenberg composed between 1902 and 1906, but also that it is more than a creative response to just this limited group of works. It holds a position of its own in the broader history of two-dimensional sonata form in the second half of the nineteenth and the early twentieth centuries, confronting the problems associated with the integration of the multi-movement pattern in a single-movement composition in an original way. Taking part in one of the most extraordinary and deeply rooted tendencies in Austro-German instrumental music of the later nineteenth and early twentieth centuries, Zemlinsky's Quartet secures its position in music history.

These conclusions will doubtlessly please all lovers of Zemlinsky's music. But are they capable of changing the canonic status of the Second Quartet? Do they add anything to Zemlinsky scholarship that has not already been observed before – by Horst Weber, Werner Loll or Antony Beaumont? To some it might seem that they do not. At first sight the analytical information presented in the above paragraphs may differ from that offered by the analyses of Weber and Loll in many details, but not in the overall tendency. And it remains to be seen whether the result of simply extending the context for the interpretation of Zemlinsky's Quartet from Schoenberg to Liszt, Strauss and others will not be restricted to the appearance of even more footnotes in studies of other works by other composers – at the very best.

There is, however, a crucial difference between this and previous analyses of Zemlinsky's Quartet. This difference does not primarily reside in the fact that it is now interpreted in an extended context, but rather in the terms in which that interpretation is cast. When Zemlinsky's Second String Quartet is analysed in a context of other works of similar formal organisation, it is not so much these other works, but rather its form that becomes its context. In this context, it becomes possible not only to analyse Zemlinsky's Quartet – as several Zemlinsky scholars have done excellently before – but also to theorise about it: to extrapolate the results of its analysis and apply them to other compositions – and vice versa. The context of large-scale instrumental music in Austro-Germany after 1850 invites the application of a terminological and conceptual apparatus to Zemlinsky's work that resonates well with a number of recent currents in scholarly thought on music that exist on the verge between music theory and musicology in the narrow sense and show a distinct interest in musical form.

Only by theorising about Zemlinsky's works does it become possible to discuss them in the same terms as we discuss acknowledged masterpieces. Only such an approach allows for the development of a discourse around Zemlinsky's music that might find broader resonance outside the fine but fairly limited circle of specialised Zemlinsky scholars. This, it seems to me, is one of the primary conditions for Zemlinsky's much overdue entry into the canon.

Notes

1   I use the terms monologic and dialogic in the sense of Mikhail Bakhtin. For instance, see Bakhtin, Mikhail (1981) *The Dialogic Imagination: Four Essays*, translated by Caryl Emerson & Michael Holquist, Austin – London: University of Texas Press.

2   Korsyn, Kevin (1999) 'Beyond Privileged Contexts: Intertextuality, Influence and Dialogue', in Nicholas Cook & Mark Everist (eds), *Rethinking Music*. Oxford: Oxford University Press, pp.55–72.

3   Klein, Michael (2005) *Intertextuality in Western Art Music*. Bloomington – Indianapolis: Indiana University Press.

4   Hepokoski, James and Warren Darcy (2006) *Elements of Sonata Theory. Norms, Types, and Deformations in the Late-Eighteenth-Century Sonata*. Oxford – New York: Oxford University Press.

5   Klein, op. cit., p.46

6   For a useful introduction, see Weber, William (1999) 'The History of Musical Canon', in Nicholas Cook & Mark Everist (eds), *Rethinking Music*. Oxford: Oxford University Press, pp.336–55.

7   Weber, Horst (1977) *Alexander Zemlinsky*, (*Österreichische Komponisten des 20. Jahrhunderts*, 23), Vienna: Lafite, pp.98–115.
    Loll, Werner (1990) *Zwischen Tradition und Avantgarde. Die Kammermusik Alexander Zemlinskys*, (*Kieler Schriften zur Musikwissenschaft*, ed. Friedhelm Krummacher & Heinrich W. Schwab, 34), Kassel: Bärenreiter, pp.133–205.
    Beaumont, Antony (2000) *Zemlinsky*. London: Faber, pp.227–40.

8   Zemlinsky, Alexander (1995) *Briefwechsel mit Arnold Schönberg, Anton Webern, Alban Berg und Franz Schreker*, ed. Horst Weber (*Briefwechsel der Wiener Schule*, ed. Thomas Ertelt, 1), Darmstadt: Wissenschaftliche Buchgesellschaft, p.97.

9   Ibid.

10 Ibid., p.127

11 I coined the term two-dimensional sonata form to replace William Newman's more familiar term double-function form. (Newman, William S (1969) *The Sonata since Beethoven*. Chapel Hill: University of North Carolina Press, p.134.) Newman's term is problematic and its definition untenable: they imply that each unit in the form has a double function – one in the sonata cycle, another in the sonata form. Given the alternation of units in which both dimensions coincide and interpolations, this is obviously not the case. It goes without saying that in this technical usage, the term two-dimensional loses every connotation of incompleteness (as opposed to three-dimensional) it might have in colloquial language.
For a detailed theoretical discussion of the concept of two-dimensional sonata form, as well as for a number of elaborate examples and a historical perspective, the reader is referred to Vande Moortele, Steven (2006) *Two-dimensional Sonata Form in Germany and Austria between 1850 and 1950. Theoretical, Analytical, and Critical Perspectives* (Ph.D. diss., University of Leuven). Compositions that are analysed as two-dimensional sonata forms in this study include Liszt's B-minor Sonata and his symphonic poems *Tasso, Les préludes,* and *Die Ideale,* Strauss's *Don Juan* and *Ein Heldenleben,* Schoenberg's *Pelleas und Melisande,* First String Quartet, and First Chamber Symphony, Zemlinsky's Second String Quartet, Franz Schreker's Chamber Symphony, and Franz Schmidt's Fourth Symphony. It is quite probable that also Suk's aforementioned Second String Quartet is in dialogue with this tradition.

12 A case in point of an approach to Zemlinsky's Quartet from within the Schoenberg context can be found in Krummacher, Friedhelm (2003) *Das Streichquartett. Teilband 2: Von Mendelssohn bis zur Gegenwart, (Handbuch der musikalischen Gattungen,* ed. Siegfried Mauser, 6,2), Laaber: Laaber Verlag, pp.256–9. Here, Zemlinsky's Second Quartet figures in a chapter entitled 'Tradition in der Krise: Schönbergs Frühwerk in seinem Kreis'.

13 Several of the analytical observations in the following paragraphs have been published before in German in Vande Moortele, Steven (2005) 'Die Funktion des Mottos in der zweidimensionalen Sonatenform bei Schönberg und Zemlinsky', in Till Knipper, Martin Kranz, Thomas Kühnrich & Carsten Neubauer (eds), *'Form follows function' – zwischen Musik, Form und Funktion. Beiträge zum 18. internationalen studentischen Symposium des DVSM,* Hamburg: Von Bockel Verlag, pp.331–41.

14 Thus, it belongs to the sentence type that Matthew BaileyShea has described as the sentence with sentential continuation. See pp.12–16 of BaileyShea, Matthew (2004) 'Beyond the Beethoven Model: Sentence Types and Limits', in *Current Musicology,* 77, pp.5–33.

Peter Fribbins

Zemlinsky's String Quartets: a Composer's View

THE TENDENCY TO MARGINALISE the works of certain composers because they inconvenience canons and historical linear paradigms is common enough: Zemlinsky can all too easily be dismissed as Schoenberg's teacher and brother-in-law, just as Frank Bridge (of the same generation) is so often marginalised as the teacher of Benjamin Britten. Horst Weber summarised the traditional view: 'Remaining open to the charge of eclecticism, [Zemlinsky] occasionally recomposed the masterpieces of his time'.[1] Nowadays one might query such readings since, in hindsight and in different ways, eclecticism has served well many later composers, Olivier Messiaen and Michael Tippett being only two such examples. After Adorno's famous 1959 essay on Zemlinsky,[2] the issue has been inextricably linked to any discussion of his work.

As a composer, I find curious the idea of 'recomposing' masterpieces, since traditionally the European composer consumes and digests the music of the past and of their time, invoking such works in the task of creating (or re-casting) an aesthetic context in which ideally, and through their individual character and voice, the music of the past may then be heard and perceived differently. Hence such remarks seem unsympathetic about, and perhaps insensitive to, creative composition and its processes.[3] Since by the end of the twentieth century a referential and intertextual sensibility had become one of the hallmarks of postmodernism, Weber may as well suggest that Zemlinsky *was ahead of his time* – that great validating (and nonsensical) claim.

In Zemlinsky's case, such pejorative judgments are unfortunately accentuated, since the overshadowing by Schoenberg tends also to be based on a set of mid twentieth-century cultural and academic values which eventually came to rate theory and system as more important than the music itself (a practice eventually prevalent in post-war Britain too, despite a natural English scepticism about theoretical systems in music). This anti-Renaissance mantra of 'theory first, sound second' was ultimately responsible for a mid twentieth-century modernism which, in its most extreme form, alienated audiences, and which contemporary composers still work to repair.

It is interesting to reflect on eclecticism if one considers Zemlinsky's music in relation to that of other composers of the time, for instance his fellow Viennese

Gustav Mahler, only eleven years older. In some ways, Mahler's aesthetic is similarly porous and intertextual, embracing and invoking the music of so many earlier classical and romantic masters, some of it hardly digested in his music at all. This referential approach and eclecticism are close bedfellows. Mahler's music, too, was marginalised until the mid twentieth century: the canon eventually presented him as a late nineteenth-century figure, transforming him into a pioneering early twentieth-century voice. Zemlinsky outlived Mahler by 31 years and so could not be presented in this way. Zemlinsky's music did not avoid the later modernism of the 1920s and 1930s, but, crucially for many twentieth-century writers, did not sufficiently adopt it, either. There are surely useful comparisons to be made with other composers born in the 1860s and 1870s. In various ways the musical reputations of Richard Strauss (b.1864), Rachmaninov (b.1873) and Respighi (b.1879) all seem to have managed to sidestep the modernist aesthetic of *absolutism* which typified mid-Europe in the middle of the twentieth century. Zemlinsky's student Erich Korngold is intriguing too: an Austrian born in 1897 could well be expected to be somewhat more radical musically, yet the growth of his popularity in recent years, at least in the performance canon, challenges the old orthodoxy of a modernist hegemony.

Hence in Zemlinsky we have a figure whose excellent music and individual voice could not be easily categorised and clearly presented in the various musical canons: he was neither arch nineteenth-century conservative, nor progressive twentieth-century radical, but resided, like most composers, somewhere between the two.[4] The twentieth-century doubts which seem to linger about Zemlinsky therefore fall essentially into two categories: first, the conservative, not moving sufficiently with the modernist times; second, the charge of 'eclecticism', an insufficiently distinctive voice of his own, and the related judgment that 'he recomposed the works of others'. I would like to test these perceptions by examining some passages from two of his quartets: Quartet No. 1 from the 1890s, when the composer was still in his twenties, and the last quartet (No. 4), from the end of his career in the 1930s.

String Quartet No. 1 in A major, Op. 4

The first quartet dates from 1896, just two years after the recently discovered Cello Sonata.[5] It was at this time that Zemlinsky met Brahms and showed him some works: upon Brahms's recommendation the quartet was then published by Simrock. Tonal identity in music as part of its discourse was clearly important in Vienna at this time: the various dark representations of D minor by the Second Viennese School composers at the turn of the twentieth century is perhaps the most common example, building on inherited key-topic principles of the Teutonic tradition. Examples include Schoenberg's 1899 *Verklärte Nacht*, Op. 4, Webern's 1908 *Passacaglia*, Op. 1 and Zemlinsky's own Symphony No. 1 from 1891 (Zemlinsky's Quartets Nos. 2 and 4 also end in D, and the end of No. 2 has clear similarities to the end of *Verklärte Nacht*).

If Mozart used A major as a key particularly for operatic love-duets, Zemlinsky's use was not dissimilar: A major was his key of joy.[6]

The first movement is a beautifully crafted and satisfying sonata-form structure, demonstrating all the competencies of a solid late nineteenth-century musical training. There are numerous traditional classical and nineteenth-century aspects to the movement. However, one of the most striking features is an impressive rhythmic suppleness and motion. This is found in motion within motifs (e.g. Violin 1, bar 1), as well as metrically, with divisions of the 6/8 time signature and conflict between the instruments, e.g. bar 3 with 6/8 and hemiolic 3/4 in the lower and upper strings respectively (Ex. 1).

Ex. 1: String Quartet No. 1 (1896) *1st movement*

This tension between duple and triple time is interesting on a number of levels: to look more closely at the music is to realise that it is not actually in a duple 6/8 at all until bar 5; *aurally* it is in triple time, but with the first violin part notated in 6/8 only in bars 1–2 and lower strings notated in 6/8 in bars 3–4. Both could equally be written in 3/4: in fact this would represent more properly the aural experience of the music. After these four bars come another four bars which are effectively in 6/8, a move from the solidity or squareness of simple time to music more lilting, dance-like and Schubertian. But, aurally and psychologically, this presents a problem since, by the end of bar 8, the listener is now presented with a certain metrical schizophrenia. The only solution possible is what Zemlinsky now provides: a direct conflict of these contrasting hemiolic worlds into a unison | 3+2+2+2+3 | 2+2+2+3 | all across the bar lines, assertive, quite dogmatic, and thoroughly rhetorical and Beethovenian. This may be reduced to a metrical formula of 2+2+2+3 again, with a 3 cell to begin, in effect a somewhat dislocated 9/8 (Ex. 1a). The two bars (12–13) which complete the first page of the 1898 Simrock edition are again marked as 6/8 but both are clearly felt as 3/4 (Ex. 1b).

Such temporal conflict is found throughout the first movement and seems to be more than the inheritance of Beethovenian motivic principles as passed on through Brahms. There is a certain Viennese logic, care and precision in the way one four-bar section is balanced metrically with another. Then there is the curious manner of notation: the sheer awkwardness of notating two against three would seem to indicate something of Zemlinsky's personal, private world of codes and ciphers, so important in his later works. Antony Beaumont draws attention to this, especially the 2+3 cells and variants of five which constitute a private signature for Zemlinsky either intervalically through pitches (e.g. D-E-G), or through rhythm and metre as in this example.[7] Schoenberg's later obsession with the intervals of minor seconds and thirds, particularly in his free atonal music post 1908 (e.g. *Drei Klavierstücke*, Op. 11, 1909), is no accident: the vertical and horizontal procedures of later Second Viennese School music are also presaged by Zemlinsky's approach. But one wonders how Brahms, in his well-documented 1896 meeting with Zemlinsky, can have been content with such notation,[8] even though the manuscript version he saw may have been the extant one (missing bar 11) and with a different bridge at bar 12.[9] Something similar seems to occur in the first movement of the newly discovered Cello Sonata: for instance in bars 10–11 there is a 3+2+3 crotchet pattern in the piano, across the bar line, conflicting with a persistent three-quaver figure in the cello, across the beats as well as the bar line (Ex. 2).

> Zemlinsky refuses to perform the act of allegiance (as Schubert did towards
> Beethoven) that would have subordinated the individual thematic shape to its function
> in the sonata-form whole.[10]

Ex. 2: Sonata for Cello and Piano (1894)

Horst Weber's commentary on the quartet's first movement is probably accurate, but his next statement, that '[e]xcept for the first violin's upbeat, the statement of the first subject in the opening bars emphasizes not the tonic but the subdominant', would seem to admit a considerable Brahmsian influence on the music. This is a common harmonic and gestural hallmark of Brahms; his symphonies alone reveal I–IV harmonic progressions in the openings of the following movements: Symphony No. 1 (movements 1, 2 and 4); Symphony No. 2 (movement 2, although this progression is in the guise of a transitory introduction in C-sharp minor); Symphony No. 3 (movements 2 and 3). This harmonic polarity becomes virtually a cliché, often, as in the chorale- or hymn-like third movement of Symphony No. 3, of a plangent or moral tone, with the religious resonances of the plagal cadence never far away. The use of the subdominant in Schubert and earlier classical composers is subtly different: Zemlinsky seems, subconsciously perhaps, to invoke either Schubert, Brahms's modification of Schubert or, probably more likely, both at once. Schubert is then *evoked* in the delicate and rather Viennese, dance-like second movement of the quartet. It also has the repeating sections which are so typical of the dances of middle movements of classical quartets and symphonies. Another interesting inheritance comes in the third movement (Ex. 3), with what seems like a clear reference to the Baroque 'French overture' style, perhaps via Schumann (I think in particular of the sharp angles and dotted rhythms of Schumann's 'Sinister Place' from *Waldscenen*, Op. 82). There is also the Baroque *invoked* through the learned manner of strict counterpoint, with contrary motion between bass and top lines, approaching an inverted contrapuntal subject. (Such serious contrapuntal procedures are found again in the astringent opening of String Quartet No. 4, in the 1930s, albeit in a rather different harmonic style.)

Ex. 3: String Quartet No. 1 (1896) *2nd movement*

Are these further fruits of a rigorous German nineteenth-century training? Reger and Zemlinsky's teacher Fuchs are surely not far away. Schumann once more echoes in the epilogue-like final ten bars of the first movement, which seem to close its narrative, just as in a Schumann character piece. The important point here is that at the age of only 25, Zemlinsky was clearly able to use tradition without being dwarfed by it. Contrary to the judgments of the twentieth century, his particular 'eclecticism' surely adds something which is quite personal and distinctive. In addition, his later music moves away from these nineteenth-century traditions, by both developing them further, and also accommodating neo-classical and modernist approaches of the 1920s and 1930s, rather as the composers of the Second Viennese School did. Zemlinsky's meetings with Brahms in 1895 and then 1896, a year before his death, may perhaps be compared to Debussy's meeting with Liszt in Rome 1885 (also a year before Liszt's death). I would suggest that Liszt made as strong an impression on Debussy as Brahms did on Zemlinsky, yet it is interesting how history seems to find it convenient to stress the Brahms meeting more than the Liszt one. The influence of Liszt's piano writing and harmonic colour is clear in Debussy's music: for instance 'Nuages' from the orchestral *Nocturnes* of the late 1890s which may be related to Liszt's *Nuages Gris* for piano (1881). Of course Debussy moved on from Liszt and other influences, just as, by 1915, Zemlinsky had moved on from that of Brahms, since his decision to conduct a Brahms symphony by that time was worthy of an ironic remark.[11]

Yet we do not so readily talk of Debussy's 'eclecticism' and the traditional, despite its clear presence. More often than not, he is presented as the first twentieth-century composer: 'one can justifiably claim that modern music began with *L'après midi d'un faune*'.[12] Zemlinsky suffers from the judgments of twentieth-century modernist writers, who subscribed to the doctrine of compositional influence, articulated through a historical, linear paradigm. His music seems marginal when stylistic 'progress' is presented as the main validating criterion, particularly in twentieth-century European music. Perhaps, then, the charge of eclecticism is not the main problem at all; it is conservatism which is the limiting issue for his musical reputation. Perhaps he was a composer of great promise in his twenties whose subsequent career failed to fulfill his potential. Hence the later music disappoints, shows lack of stylistic development and engagement with the *lingua franca* of the new twentieth century. In this case, it would be useful to examine the last string quartet rather than the first.

String Quartet No. 4, Op. 25

The fourth quartet (1936) takes the form of a suite in six movements and was composed as a tribute to his friend Alban Berg who had died at the end of the previous year. The opening is remarkable: astringent in its harmony, simple in rhythm and direct in musical gesture (Ex. 4). It intimates both a sombre chorale as well as earlier contrapuntal procedure. Aesthetically, it is not far from Berg, Stravinsky and Hindemith, while in technical terms it evokes Baroque and Renaissance contrapuntal masters.

Ex. 4: String Quartet No. 4 (1936) *1st movement* PRÄLUDIUM

Temporally, the opening again seems to show a set of personal cipher preoccupations, particularly with twos and threes which connect it with the first quartet from forty years before: three crotchets followed by two more in the first two bars, then in predominantly shorter values with three quavers/crotchets followed by two and then shorter still with quaver/semiquaver movement up to bar 6. This tension-building telescopic effect is thoroughly Beethovenian, and I wonder if he had in mind the famous example of the opening of Beethoven's F minor Piano Sonata, Op. 2, No. 1:

Ex.5: Sonata in F Minor, Op. 2, No. I – Beethoven

The linear signature is then followed in bar 6 with a vertical one in pitches, as the first violin, hitherto silent, intones, somewhat mournfully, the D-E-G motif (Ex. 4a). Using the same pitches, this signature also opened String Quartet No. 2 (1914). Bar 9 is curious since the violin's unison is not particularly idiomatic string quartet writing; however perhaps the gesture of 'coming together' is somehow more important than the sound; the opening is certainly far from the classical model and style of String Quartet No. 1, but at the same time the music is essentially in E minor, and the whole movement ends on a 'transfigured' E major chord, high above the dirge-like motif of the opening. That Zemlinsky can embrace such a wide range and link such apparently diverse techniques is one of the most impressive aspects of his approach and style in this piece: from the use of tonality and a somewhat conventional use of key signatures, to more modernist motivic and asymmetrical procedures; and from highly personalised solo moments (e.g. the cello solo in the *Barcarole*) to the more formal (and traditional) double fugue of the Finale.

If the quartet relates in some way to Berg's *Lyric Suite* (1926),[13] that work itself relates to Zemlinsky's *Lyric Symphony* (1922). Hence a discussion of 'eclecticism' fails to take account of the tendency of Viennese composers of this time to quote and refer to each other's works as well as the masterworks of the past. Besides cipher relationships, the broader intertextual tendency sometimes verged on the obsessive and was a defining post-Mahlerian feature of Expressionism and the aesthetic of the Second Viennese School. It is surely in this local historical and aesthetic context that the assertion of 'recomposing' the works of others needs to be judged. With a twenty-first-century perspective that tends more equivocally to contextualise and rationalise the disparate cultural epoch of the twentieth century, it may be that a work like the Fourth String Quartet – which presents a seemingly unified aesthetic through a wide and inclusive set of techniques – can be seen to be the precursor to polystylism and other postmodernist approaches.[14] In other words, our historical judgments are already inevitably moving away from the values of twentieth-century modernism to be replaced by another, still to be described. This can do no harm to Zemlinsky's future reputation.

Notes

1   Weber, Horst (1980) 'Zemlinsky', in *New Grove Dictionary of Music & Musicians*, Vol. 20 (ed. S Sadie). London: Macmillan, pp.665–6.

2   Adorno, TW (1994) 'Zemlinsky' [1963] in R Livingstone (trans.) *Quasi una Fantasia*. London and New York: Verso, pp.111–29.

3   In this context a more sensitive discussion of this issue can be found in Puffett, Derrick (1996) 'Transcription & recomposition: the strange case of Zemlinsky's Maeterlinck songs', in *Analytical strategies and musical interpretation* (ed. Craig Ayrey & Mark Everist). Cambridge: CUP, pp.72–119.

4   One might argue for degrees of strength of voice and significance in different canons. For example Debussy was a highly original, early twentieth-century voice in piano and orchestral music in particular. However, in the string chamber music canon his presence is slender: there is only the early quartet from 1893 and the late cello and violin sonatas. The problem for Zemlinsky, who is much more significant in string chamber works, is that this particular canon, and quartets especially (as I know from my own compositional experience), is perhaps the hardest of all in which to compete.

5   Premiered in the UK by Raphael Wallfisch (cello) & John York (piano) at Middlesex University, 11 October 2006 in the Conference 'Zemlinsky, Lost & Found'.

6   Beaumont, Antony (2000) *Zemlinsky*, London: Faber. p.52.

7   Ibid. pp.197–208

8   Brahms's own cypheric tendencies are open to speculation. For instance the temporal tensions at the opening of his Third Symphony with pedantically notated (but unheard) tied duplets that indicate a 6/4 metre, seemingly symbolic since they are followed by music which is clearly aurally in 3/2. Also, the F-A(b)-F bass line *Frei aber froh* – 'free but happy' – is a personal signature in the lower strings.

9   This first page of the manuscript is reproduced in the booklet to the recording of the quartets made by the LaSalle Quartet (Deutsche Grammophon, 1982).

10 Weber, Horst (1982) 'Uber Zemlinskys Streichquartette' [1977], CD notes to LaSalle
    Quartet's recording of Zemlinsky's string quartets, Deutsche Grammophon 2741 016,
    pp.5–9.

11 Beaumont, op. cit., p.35

12 Boulez, Pierre (1991) 'Chapter IV, Entries for a Musical Encyclopaedia (Debussy)' [1958],
    in Stephen Walsh (trans.) *Stocktakings from an Apprenticeship*. Oxford: Clarendon, p.267.

13 Horst Weber, op. cit., p.17

14 Michael Musgrave makes a similar claim for Brahms, albeit via an argument concerning
    reception. See Musgrave, Michael (2000) *Toward a New Evaluation: Brahms the
    Postmodernist*, A Brahms Reader. New Haven, Connecticut: Yale, pp.283–6.

Appendix

Lecture–Recital: Zemlinsky and the Forgotten Late Romantic Composers of Lieder

Jane Manning

As AHRC Research Fellow at Kingston University, Jane Manning is currently researching the performance and legacy of the Sprechstimme *of Schoenberg's* Pierrot lunaire, *a crucial landmark in the history of vocal music. As part of the background to her research, she has been tapping into the richly rewarding and much-neglected vein of late romantic song that preceded* Pierrot lunaire, *including, of course, Schoenberg's own significant contribution to the lieder repertoire. At the Middlesex University Zemlinsky Conference, with Terence Allbright (piano), she gave a Lecture–Recital of lieder by Zemlinsky and his contemporaries. An edited text of her lecture is given here, including her comments on the items in the programme along with her translations of the Zemlinsky works she performed: the* Six Waltz Songs, Op. 6 *and* Six Maeterlinck Songs, Op.13.

It is my firm belief that Zemlinsky and his contemporaries would find a regular place in recital programmes if they were more widely known and, especially, promoted more effectively, for audiences for lieder are sometimes less open-minded than they could be. They are cultured and knowledgeable up to a point, but they occasionally betray elements of self-congratulatory nostalgia verging even on snobbery. I have never been able to understand why, amongst twentieth-century composers, the entire outputs of Richard Strauss and Mahler are regarded as readily accessible while the early songs of Schoenberg and Berg are not. Closer knowledge of the music would prove otherwise. Strauss's varied and plentiful lieder do, of course, flatter the voice and make a gratifying and instant impression on audiences and audition panels. Though some of his less familiar songs, such as the *Lieder der Ophelia*, Op. 67 (1918) are attractively quirky and challenging, others, including many popular favourites, can seem to veer dangerously towards sentimentality.

Schoenberg seems to remain, most unfairly – indeed outrageously – the bogeyman to those who know virtually nothing of his vocal output. The pleasure of Schoenberg's meticulous vocal writing will, sadly, remain unknown to those determined to reject it out of hand. Doubtless Zemlinsky's connection with Schoenberg has not helped his cause (though promoting less-known romantic lieder should not be an excuse for avoiding anything more modern). In my view, the perfect marriage of words and music achieved by Hugo Wolf in the craft of lieder-writing is matched most notably by the figures of the Second Viennese School and their less well-known forebears, including Zemlinsky. Singers know from experience what lies well in the voice and when texts are set so that they are easily placed and articulated. Some Schubert songs, though easy on the ear, do not always feel comfortable. Strophic songs, in particular, can throw up some awkward, strangulating moments when vowels have to be modified and strenuous efforts made to avoid being throttled by close successions of syllables high in the range – not to mention impracticable phrase-lengths. I can assert from long experience that Schoenberg and Webern songs often sit more easily in the voice than some favourites by Schubert or Brahms (Schubert's 'Gretchen am Spinnrade' is a particular challenge for young voices, especially at its climax which is full of closed vowels on high pitches). Coping with the musical demands is, of course, an entirely separate matter.

To discover a bountiful supply of relatively unfamiliar lieder is a special delight. It oxygenates some of the more faded corners of the genre, affording a prime opportunity for a fresh approach from a modern perspective, unhindered by the weight of tradition and habit. Those who guide young singers must always be willing to encourage them to seek out new pieces. It is all too easy to revolve on the spot, coaching only those works one knows intimately already, without troubling to entertain any new thoughts on them. I have the impression that, as can be noted in performances of Gilbert and Sullivan operettas, conventions of performing German lieder can become set in stone, and may need pickaxe treatment to free them. The special appeal of the less-known Austro-German lieder is that they combine the features of late-romantic *fin-de-siècle* Vienna and Berlin, its Expressionism and Symbolism, with subtle glimpses into future modernism. The choice of poets is exceptionally stimulating and often inspired by the spirit of the time. It is a joy to negotiate such flexible and shapely lines, with all nuances and dynamics sensitively judged. Phrases are of a practicable length and words are set with precision, aiding clarity of diction and understanding of their meaning. All singers and teachers should welcome the works of Zemlinsky and his contemporaries.

FRANZ SCHREKER (1878–1934)

Frühling (No. 2 from *5 Lieder*, Op. 4)

Schreker is a major song composer who deserves a prime place in the repertoire. He was born in Monaco to a much-travelled family of Bohemian, German-speaking Jewish origin (though his father converted to Protestantism and his mother was a Catholic). As conductor of the Vienna Philharmonic Chorus he promoted the works of Schoenberg, with whom he struck up a good friendship, and those of Mahler, Debussy, and even Delius and Cyril Scott – and, of course, Zemlinsky. Schreker wrote his own libretti for his operas for which he is primarily known, in particular *Der Ferne Klang*, premiered in Frankfürt in 1912. He had a great influence on composers of a later generation such as Berg, Weill and Krenek. Appointed Head of the Berlin Hochschule in 1920 he was later denounced by Hitler and removed from his post. His music was banned, and the resultant trauma induced a heart attack so that, unlike many of his contemporaries, he did not manage to emigrate. His career was therefore confined to the German-speaking world, and he was virtually forgotten at the time of his death.

He wrote many fine songs in lyrical, romantic vein, most dating from his student days. His *Lieder* Op. 5 form a delicious cycle that any soprano or tenor should relish.

Entführung

This song probably dates from 1909, but it was not published until 1912; it is rather more forward-looking in style and flexibility of expression than 'Frühling'. Significantly, the poem is by Stefan George (1868–1933), the symbolist poet most beloved of Schoenberg and his circle, but this is Schreker's only George setting.

Happily, all of Schreker's vocal music is now readily available, thanks to the splendid efforts of the Schreker Foundation.

JOSEF MARX (1882–1964)

Like Schreker, Marx, another important Austrian songwriter of the period, enjoyed early success but later faded from the limelight. He was prolific and impressive but highly conservative in his musical inclinations, and no friend to Schoenberg. He even published a treatise on musical Vienna which made no reference to Schoenberg or Berg. He was a Director of the Vienna Hochschule and critic for the *Wiener Zeitung*, and finally became Head of the new Turkish Conservatory in Ankara.

It is interesting that Marx made settings of four of Otto Hartleben's translations of the *Pierrot* poems not long before Schoenberg embarked on his masterpiece. The songs have exceptionally virtuosic and elaborate piano parts and the vocal writing evokes the world of cabaret. Two of them set verses featured in *Pierrot lunaire*. When I discovered Marx's 'Pierrot Dandy' (1910) I assumed it to be a setting of the same poem as No. 3 of *Pierrot lunaire* – 'Der Dandy'. In fact it is another poem by Hartleben, one that does not appear in any anthology. It describes a similar scene – that of Pierrot at his toilette – but in different words, and it contains an oblique reference to Pierrot's beloved Columbine. *Valse de Chopin* indeed uses the same poem as No. 5 of *Pierrot lunaire*, and there is plenty of Viennese *schmaltz* in keeping with the text.

Kolumbine

The poem is familiar in its setting as the second movement of *Pierrot lunaire*. Marx's version was written in 1911, a year before Schoenberg's. Schoenberg has a much more detailed approach to the words in his chosen medium of *sprechstimme*. One wonders if Schoenberg heard this song and decided to employ an entirely different metre – an ingeniously skewed waltz rhythm, blurring the bar-lines – in contrast to Marx's rather more straightforward choice, despite his considerable demands on the pianist.

ARNOLD SCHOENBERG (1874–1951)

Saget Mir (*Das Büch der Hängenden Gärten,* Op. 15, No. 5)

This is a brief extract from Schoenberg's masterly song-cycle which was written in 1908/9. The complete work is a substantial, fifteen-movement piece, which well illustrates Schoenberg's preoccupation with detail; it yields huge rewards from repeated hearings and is wonderfully satisfying to work on. It teaches one a great deal about placing of the voice and acute responsiveness to Stefan George's evocative texts.

ALEXANDER ZEMLINSKY (1871–1942)

Translations by Jane Manning of the texts of the two Zemlinsky song-cycles are given below.

Six Waltz Songs, Op. 6

These charming 'lollipops' date from 1898 and are representative of Zemlinsky's earliest style, with echoes of Brahms; they are, of course, entirely tonal. The German texts are by Ferdinand Gregorovius (1821–1891), who used, as a basis, an anonymous collection of Tuscan folk poetry.

The songs are wistful and romantic in tone with the startling exception of No. 4, 'Ich gehe des Nachts', which seems to be almost a microcosm of Schoenberg's mighty monodrama *Erwartung*, Op. 17, of 1909, in which a woman searches vainly at night for her lover, fearing the worst. It is brief and eerie and is in a lower tessitura than the others.

Sechs Gesänge, Op. 13

This cycle of Six Songs to poems by Maeterlinck was written between 1910 and 1913, and is rightly considered one of Zemlinsky's finest works. The symbolist poet Maurice Maeterlinck (1862–1949) was, like Albert Giraud (author of the original *Pierrot* poems) a French-speaking Belgian whose best-known works include 'The

Bluebird' and *Pelléas et Mélisande*, as well as a treatise on the life of the bee. His texts, including these poems, portray a world of exotic fable and dark fairytale, with disturbing undertones of mystery and impending doom.

Zemlinsky seems to have experienced some tension in trying to blend his earlier 'classical' style with the more radical developments happening around him. The last song in particular shows signs of this: throughout, tempi and dynamics are subtly and constantly fluctuating and there are some distinctly unexpected shifts of tonality.

There are all kinds of intonation traps in this highly chromatic idiom and the performer is constantly put to the test of achieving perfect tuning. Detailed and precise dynamic markings enhance the intensity of the experience.

The composer pours a wealth of meaning into the terse, understated texts with their sinister resonances. The combination of late romanticism with a rather tentative modernism makes the cycle especially fascinating and compelling. The first and last songs have a quasi-Mahlerian marching tread and folksong elements are also evident, with their repeated refrains. The third is still, rapt and contemplative, in contrast to the general restlessness of the others, while the fifth bears an uncanny resemblance to Frank Bridge's rarely heard song 'What shall I your true love tell?'

FRANK BRIDGE (1879–1941)

What shall I your true love tell?

This song was published in 1919 and sets a poem by Francis Thompson. Bridge was more cosmopolitan in outlook than some of his English contemporaries and is quite likely to have heard Zemlinsky's Op. 13 songs. The subject-matter itself and the actual treatment of this death-bed dialogue, with its contrasting voices and modal melodic basis, are so extraordinarily similar to Op. 13, No. 5 that it can hardly be coincidence.

Another interesting link between Zemlinsky and Bridge is that both composers wrote settings of poems by the Indian poet Rabindranath Tagore (1861–1941), the former in his *Lyric Symphony* (1923), and the latter in his last songs 'Day after day' (1922), 'Speak to me, my love' (1924) and 'Dweller in my deathless dreams' (1925), the first two of which were also orchestrated by the composer. (Tagore was winner of the Nobel Prize for Literature in 1913 and undertook a triumphant European tour in 1921[1]).

Notes

1   See Beaumont, A (2000) *Zemlinsky*. London: Faber, p.313–18.

ALEXANDER VON ZEMLINSKY (1871–1942)

6 WALZER-GESÄNGE, Op. 6 *(Waltz Songs)*

German texts by Ferdinand Gregorovius, based on traditional Tuscan songs.
(Translations by Jane Manning)
© Jane Manning

Liebe Schwalbe *(Dear swallow)*

Dear swallow, you take wing and sing so early,
Weaving your sweet melody all over the blue sky.
Those who sleep late in the morning, all the lovers at rest,
With your twittering song you awaken the slumbering ones.

Get up, get up, you sleeping lovers, now that the morning swallow calls you!
For the night will cheat you of rest if you waste the daylight in sleep.

Klagen ist der Mond gekommen *(The moon arrives complaining)*

The moon arrives complaining at the glare of the sun's face.
Heaven ought still to bless her,
Even if you rob her of light and radiance.

She is bent on counting her stars, and is ready to die of grief.
Two of her prettiest stars are missing,
Those that now shine in your face.

Fensterlein, nachts bist du zu *(Little window, at night you are closed)*

Little window, at night you are closed,
In the daytime you revive my sorrow.
You are fringed with carnations,
O! Open now, delight of my eye!

Window of precious stone,
Sunshine within and stars outside.
O little window, snug and small,
Sunshine within and roses outside

Ich gehe des Nachts (I wander at night)

I wander at night following the moon's trail,
I look for the place where they have taken my beloved.
I saw Death there, the Dark One.
He said: 'Do not search. I have buried him'.
I wander at night following the moon's trail.
I look for the place where they have taken my beloved.

Blaues Sternlein (Little blue star)

Little blue star, please be quiet, do not give away the secret.
You must not show everyone our unspoken bond of love.
Others can remain steeped in gloom, and each can say what they will.
We are content for our two hearts to stay in this state of silent bliss.

Briefchen schrieb' ich (I wrote messages).

I wrote messages and tossed them away in the wind.
They fell into the sea and on the sand.
I secured them with chains of snow and ice,
And now the sun melts them in my hand.

Maria, Maria, you must know that he who stays the course wins in the end.
Maria, you have to believe this:
He who persists to eternity will triumph!

ALEXANDER (VON) ZEMLINSKY: (1871–1942)

6 GESÄNGE Op. 13 (Maeterlinck) 1910–1913

(Translation by Jane Manning)
© Jane Manning

Die Drei Schwestern (The three sisters)

The three sisters wished to die, and put on their golden crowns.
They went to fetch Death – they fancied he lived in the woods.
'Forest, if you grant our wish to die, you can inherit three golden crowns '.
Then the forest began to laugh, and, with a thousand kisses,
It divulged to them the future.

The three sisters wished to die, and fancied they would find Death in the sea, So made a three-year pilgrimage there.
'Sea, if you let us die, you shall inherit three golden crowns.'
Then the sea began to weep, and, with three hundred kisses,
Told them of the past.

The three sisters wished to die.
They turned their steps towards the town that lay in the middle of an island. 'Town, if you allow us to die, you shall inherit three golden crowns.'
And the town opened its gates, and, with passionate loving kisses,
Told them of the present.

Die Mädchen mit den verbundenen Augen (The girls with their eyes bound)

The girls with their eyes bound (take off the golden bandages!),
Wished to find their destiny.
At midday (leave the golden bandages on!)
They opened the castle in the meadow.
They greeted life (pull the golden bandages tighter!)
But found no way out.
The girls with their eyes bound,
Wished to find their destiny.

Lied der Jungfrau (Song of the virgin)

To all weeping souls, all afflicted with gnawing guilt,
I open my hands full of grace, wreathed with stars.

All guilt comes to nothing before love's prayer.
No soul that weeps and pleads can die.
Love loses its way in earthly fields;
Tears show me its trail.

Als ihr Geliebter schied (When her beloved went away)

When her beloved went away (I heard the door close),
I saw her weeping.
But when he came back (I saw the lamp glow),
Another was there.
And I saw Death, (I felt his breath),
And I saw Death, awaiting him also.

Und kehrt er einst heim (And if he returns home one day)

And if he returns home one day, what should I say to him?
'Say, I waited till life ran out'.
If he keeps asking and fails to recognise me immediately?
'Speak to him like a sister… perhaps he will be suffering.'
If he should ask where you are, what should I tell him?
'Give him my gold ring and see him struck dumb.'
Will he want to know why the house is so deserted?
'Show him the open door – say the Light went out'.
And when if he enquires further about the last hour?
'Say, for fear he might weep, that my lips were smiling'.

Sie kam zum Schloß gegangen (She came to the castle)

She came to the castle (the sun was hardly up).
She came to the castle, and the knights looked on in fear…
And the women fell silent.
She stopped in front of the gate (the sun was hardly up).
She stopped in front of the gate.
The Queen was heard leaving, and the King asked her,
'Where are you going? (Take care in the twilight) – where are you going?
Is there anyone waiting for you down there?'
She said neither yes nor no.
She went down to the stranger (Take care in the twilight).
She went down to the stranger, and clasped her in her arms.
The two of them said not a word and hurried off together.

About the contributors

Antony Beaumont, known primarily as a Zemlinsky and Busoni specialist, is also a practical musician of considerable versatility. As a child he studied violin, viola, piano and organ, and at the age of sixteen was already making his name as conductor, composer, arranger, writer and broadcaster. He read music at Cambridge, where he also gained his first experience of symphonic and operatic conducting. Subsequently he worked as an orchestral violinist in London before settling into an operatic career in Switzerland and Germany. In 1990 he abandoned his theatre career to spend more time researching and writing. Recently he has turned his attention, both as researcher and performer, to Weill, Wolpe and Manfred Gurlitt. In a repertoire ranging from early baroque to 20th-century avant-garde, he has recorded for the Capriccio, Koch International and Chandos labels.

Raymond Coffer has an unusual background for an academic. For well over twenty years he was a successful manager of 'alternative' rock bands (Smashing Pumpkins, Cocteau Twins, The Sundays, Love and Rockets, Ian McCulloch, among others). Around the millennium, his lifelong fascination with Viennese *fin-de-siècle* culture led him to research the Expressionist artist Richard Gerstl, now the subject of his doctoral thesis at the Institute of Germanic and Romance Studies, University of London. Coffer has translated thousands of letters and documents, many hitherto unseen, in the course of his research, and his chapter on Zemlinsky touches on a small portion of these.

Christopher Dromey is Lecturer in Music and Leader of the BA Music & Arts Management course at Middlesex University. He also teaches at the Open University and Birkbeck College, University of London. His forthcoming doctoral thesis on *The Pierrot Ensembles* (King's College, London) traces the British-led repertory of works derived from Arnold Schoenberg's *Pierrot lunaire*. He has published on the music of Elisabeth Lutyens and Sir Peter Maxwell Davies, and was previously Repertoire Researcher for the Performing Right Society (PRS).

Peter Fribbins is a composer, Director of Music at Middlesex University, and Artistic Director of the London Chamber Music Series based at Kings Place. He studied composition at the Royal Academy of Music and with Hans Werner Henze in

London and Italy. His works are varied and widely performed and he is particularly known for string chamber music. This includes two quartets (for the Allegri and Chilingirian Quartets), a Cello Sonata (for Raphael Wallfisch and John York), a Clarinet Quintet, and a Piano Trio (commissioned by the Austrian government and premiered in Vienna in 2004). His recent 'Softly in the dusk...', inspired by D.H. Lawrence, illustrates the close affinity his work often has with poetry and prompted *The Independent* to call him 'one of the outstanding composers of his generation.'

Michael Frith is an organist, composer and academic. He has performed widely in Britain and in Europe as a soloist and accompanist, and among his compositions are a considerable number of short choral works which have been extensively performed world-wide, two large-scale works for chorus and orchestra, a Clarinet Sonata, a Viola Concerto and an Organ Symphony. His most recent articles and papers are on Franck's *Trois Chorals* and recordings of organ improvisations. His current research is in the field of nineteenth- and early twentieth-century French organ music; he is a Visiting Lecturer in Music at Middlesex University.

Shoko Hino is a pianist, teaching assistant and doctoral candidate at the University of Missouri at Kansas City, Conservatory of Music. She has received several awards, including the Lorraine Watson and Hubert Chartrand Piano Scholarships, a Women's Council Scholarship and the Musica Nova Scholarship, and was a prizewinner in the Boca Raton Pops Competition and finalist at the National Society of Arts and Letters Competition. In 2007 she was awarded the UMKC School of Graduate Studies Dissertation Research Fellowship Grant. Entitled 'The Magic of Rhythm: Application of Dalcroze Eurhythmics in the Piano Lesson', her thesis discusses the incorporation of Dalcroze technique into the private piano lessons at the college level.

Jane Manning's career has covered a wide repertoire and the world's leading festivals and concert halls: Bach under Richter, Salieri under Harnoncourt, major operatic roles by Mozart, Purcell, Lully, Britten and Weill, and many BBC broadcasts. Known especially as an interpreter of contemporary music, she has given more than 350 world premières, working with Bennett, Birtwistle, Boulez, Cage, Carter, Davies, Knussen and Weir, among others. Her extensive discography includes the major song cycles of Messiaen, all Satie's vocal music, and works by Berg, Dallapiccola, Ligeti and Schoenberg with conductors such as Boulez and Rattle. Manning began performance-based research on Schoenberg's *Pierrot lunaire* as AHRC Creative Arts Fellow at Kingston University in 2004: a two-volume study of the work's vocal part will soon be published by Southern Voices. She also contributes to the forthcoming *History of Musical Performance* (CUP), and is author of two books on *New Vocal Repertory*. Awarded the OBE in 1990, Manning holds Honorary Doctorates from Durham, York and Keele Universities and is Fellow of the Royal Academy and Royal College of Music.

David Smith is Head of Opera and Choral studies at the University of KwaZulu-Natal, in Durban, South Africa, having been lecturer in music theory from 1989 to 2003. He is an experienced chamber pianist and continuo player, as well as a choral conductor. His research interests are directed at the social contexts of music – in particular, questions of colonial history.

Pamela Tancsik is a Lecturer at the Opera Studio & Choral Academy, University of KwaZulu-Natal. In 2007 she was awarded a postdoctoral research scholarship for the South African music archive project (SAMAP) by the National SA Research Fund. Her research topic: Tracing Joseph Trauneck, a Schoenberg pupil who emigrated in 1934 from Germany to South Africa and founded the Johannesburg Symphony Orchestra. She completed her PhD in opera history at the Munich Ludwig Maximilians University in 1997. Her thesis *Die Prager Oper heißt Zemlinsky. Theatergeschichte des Neuen Deutschen Theaters Prag in der Ära Alexander Zemlinsky 1911–1927* was published in Vienna in 2000. A translation of the book in Czech is planned for 2011.

Steven Vande Moortele studied musicology at the University of Leuven as well as at the Technische Universität Berlin, and obtained his doctoral degree at the University of Leuven in 2006 with a dissertation on 'Two-dimensional Sonata Form in Germany and Austria between 1850 and 1950'. Currently, he is a postdoctoral research fellow of the Research Foundation, Flanders based at the University of Leuven, spending the next academic year as a visiting scholar at the Schulich School of Music of McGill University (Montreal). He is particularly interested in *Formenlehre* and the analysis of large-scale instrumental music from the late eighteenth and nineteenth centuries, as well as in the music of the second Viennese School.

Philip Weller is a Lecturer at the University of Nottingham. His research has ranged widely through music of the later nineteenth and early twentieth century, focusing in particular on the poetics of opera and more generally on questions of musical aesthetics. He has also written on a variety of critical, historical and historiographical topics in medieval and renaissance music. His recent publications include studies of Symbolist opera (Dukas, Debussy, Bartók, Schoenberg), of French musical poetics (Debussy and Segalen), and of Messiaen. He has published on performance practice and on Viennese music (Johannes Brahms, Franz Schmidt) in collaboration with Professor Robert Pascall. Other research interests are in the fields of music and language (including the related topics of the *lied* and *mélodie*) and the philosophy of musical experience and performance. A skilled linguist, he has also worked extensively as a translator and reciter.

Index